Quality Management Fundamentals

Steven M. Bragg

AccountingTools®

Published by AccountingTools, Inc., Centennial, Colorado.

No part of this publication may be reproduced, stored in a retrieval system, or transmitted in any form or by any means, except as permitted under Section 107 or 108 of the 1976 United States Copyright Act, without the prior written permission of the Publisher. Requests to the Publisher for permission should be addressed to Steven M. Bragg, 6727 E. Fremont Place, Centennial, CO 80112.

ISBN 978-1-64221-202-0

For more information about AccountingTools® products, visit our Web site at www.accountingtools.com.

Table of Contents

About the Author

Steven Bragg, CPA, has been the chief financial officer or controller of four companies, as well as a consulting manager at Ernst & Young. He received a master's degree in finance from Bentley College, an MBA from Babson College, and a Bachelor's degree in Economics from the University of Maine. He has been a two-time president of the Colorado Mountain Club, and is an avid alpine skier, mountain biker, and certified master diver. Mr. Bragg resides in Centennial, Colorado. He has written more than 300 books and courses, including *New Controller Guidebook*, *GAAP Guidebook*, and *Payroll Management*.

Steven maintains the accountingtools.com web site, which contains continuing professional education courses, the Accounting Best Practices podcast, and thousands of articles on accounting subjects.

Buy Additional AccountingTools Courses

AccountingTools offers more than 1,500 hours of CPE courses, with concentrations in accounting, auditing, finance, taxation, and ethics. Related courses that you might like include:

- Constraint Management
- Inventory Management
- Operations Management

Go to accountingtools.com/cpe to view these additional courses.

AccountingTools®

Chapter 1
Overview of Quality Management

Introduction

Quality refers to the extent to which a product is free of deficiencies. It can also be taken to mean the conformance of a product to the requirements for it. The discussions of quality within this book will meld the two concepts together, where quality is considered to be the deficiency-free conformance of a product to the requirements for it. In this chapter, we discuss the essentials of quality management, including the types of quality, how it is managed, and how its cost is identified and reported.

Types of Quality

What is product quality? A customer perceives a product as having a high level of quality if it conforms to his or her expectations. Thus, high quality is really just making sure that a product does what a customer expects it to do.

EXAMPLE

Rapunzel Hair Products has designed a comb made of titanium, and markets it as a light weight product for the frequent traveler. Not only is the comb made of titanium, but it is also stamped with the world-famous RHR logo, and has a special low-friction coating that keeps hair tangles from being trapped in the comb. It sells for $20, and costs $16 to manufacture. The margin is unacceptably low, so the product manager is searching for ways to reduce the cost.

He surveys comb owners, and finds that their perception of quality is not that the comb is made of titanium, but simply that it is light weight. After some research, the product manager finds that titanium is twice as strong as aluminum, but is 60% heavier than that metal. Product testing reveals that aluminum is sufficiently strong to prevent bending. Aluminum is also ten times less expensive than titanium.

Consequently, Rapunzel changes the composition of the comb to an all-aluminum version that it can produce (with some extra heat tempering steps) for just $4. Since the weight of the product has declined, customers perceive the comb to have a higher quality level than the titanium version.

Based on this definition, quality is *not* having the highest possible standards for creating the ultimate product. Thus, if management insists on creating a mahogany interior for a car's glove box when the customer only wants it to be big enough to store documents, then it has just gone to considerable expense to create something that a customer does not define as being of high quality. Conversely, if the customer expects a car's steering wheel to be heated and it is not, then there is an adverse gap between customer expectations and what is being provided – which is an opportunity for improvement.

This view of quality means that a company can eliminate any costs that customers have no quality perceptions about. The cost reduction can impact a great many areas. For example, it may be perfectly acceptable to use lower-quality or thinner materials, or to allow blemishes in areas where customers cannot see them, or to allow production at a lower tolerance level than is currently the case (which eliminates some rework costs).

There are two types of quality that a company should be concerned about, one of which originates in the engineering department, while the other is the responsibility of the entire organization. They are:

- *Quality of design.* This is the ability of a company to design a product that conforms to the quality expectations of a customer. In other words, the quality that customers expect is designed into the product. This type of quality requires a considerable amount of interpretation of what engineers think customers want, and how these wishes are integrated into the final product design. If quality is not designed into the basic structure of a product, there is no way to improve the quality situation later, short of replacing the product with a new version.
- *Quality of conformance.* This is the ability of a company to produce a product that conforms to the original product design. This type of quality is not just the responsibility of the production department; the procurement staff has to acquire the correct materials, the shipping department must deliver it without damage, and the marketing department must communicate the attributes of the product that matter most to customers.

EXAMPLE

Rapunzel Hair Products wants to create a hair straightener for women who travel frequently. A survey of such travelers reveals that their views of quality for such a product encompass light weight, the ability to operate at different voltages, a variable temperature setting, and a power cord that will not break or pull away from the unit.

Of these four quality issues, three are entirely design issues – the engineering staff must design for low weight, a variable voltage capability, and a variable temperature setting. Only one of the quality issues is entirely a quality of conformance issue, which is the power cord. The purchasing department must obtain a sufficiently robust power cord to ensure that it will not break.

The quality of conformance does have a secondary role in ensuring the quality of this product, however. The procurement staff must be sure to acquire power transformers and temperature rheostats that will continue to work properly for a long period of rough handling.

Quality in the Organizational Hierarchy

Since quality must be dealt with across an organization, it will be necessary for the managers of all departments to work together to achieve enhanced quality levels. This means that senior management will need to be involved, to ensure that all departments work together in a coordinated manner. However, diffusing responsibility for quality across the organization is not sufficient – there needs to be a formal position at the vice president level for a quality manager. The parties reporting to this position are noted in the following exhibit.

Quality Organizational Structure

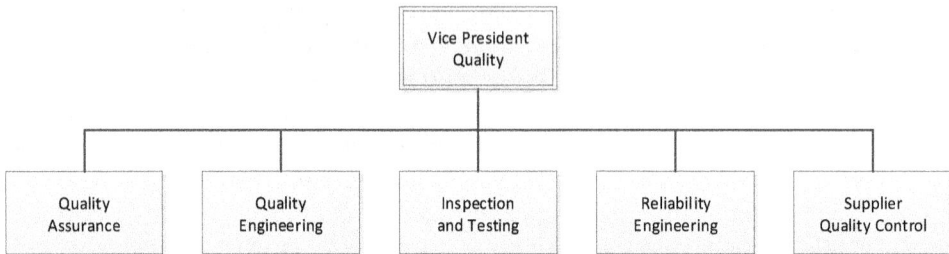

```
                    ┌──────────────────┐
                    │  Vice President  │
                    │     Quality      │
                    └──────────────────┘
        ┌──────────┬──────────┼──────────┬──────────┐
 ┌──────────┐┌──────────┐┌──────────┐┌──────────┐┌──────────┐
 │ Quality  ││ Quality  ││Inspection││Reliability││ Supplier │
 │Assurance ││Engineering││and Testing││Engineering││Quality Control│
 └──────────┘└──────────┘└──────────┘└──────────┘└──────────┘
```

In the preceding organizational structure, the quality assurance group is responsible for writing quality-related procedures and maintaining a quality manual, while also conducting quality training and performing quality audits. The quality engineering group is responsible for establishing quality standards, testing equipment, and analyzing rejected materials. The inspection and testing group is responsible for both in-process and final product inspection and testing, as well as maintaining inspection records. The reliability engineering group is responsible for setting reliability goals, conducting stress analyses, selecting suppliers, and maintaining the failure reporting and corrective action system. Finally, the supplier quality control group is responsible for evaluating supplier quality information systems and conducting supplier inspections.

A major concern within a traditionally-organized hierarchical decision structure is that decision-making tends to be segregated within departmental silos. This means that some department managers will attend to quality issues better than others, resulting in varying levels of process and product quality across an organization. It is usually not possible to impose a proper degree of attention to quality across all of these silos. Instead, it will be necessary to adopt a different organizational structure that employs cross-functional teams. These teams are empowered by senior management to impose decisions on the entire organization regarding policy goals, and will also ensure that those policies are followed.

It might seem that the imposition of cross-functional quality teams would create a burdensome additional expense for a business, perhaps resulting in the loss of a significant amount of profitability. But, when managed effectively, these teams can achieve the reverse, producing higher-quality products and processes that customers are willing to pay for. A business might elect to re-invest these extra profits back into the business, resulting in more innovative products that will attract even more customers. Alternatively, management might elect to offer the same prices as the competition, and build market share as customers realize that they can obtain higher quality from the company at the same price being charged for competing products. Higher market share allows a business to obtain cost reductions through volume purchases, which in turn increases its profits. In short, either approach will allow a business to use quality as a competitive tool to enhance its profits.

> **Note:** A further advantage of offering higher-quality products is that customers will seek out the firm in the future to make repeat purchases, which means that the business will need to spend less on marketing activities to increase its sales.

Within the traditional hierarchical organizational structure, quality was considered to be the responsibility of a separate group of quality personnel, who were tasked with verifying that products conformed to customer requirements – with inspections scheduled just prior to the point of shipment. This approach merely caught low-quality products after they had already been produced, so that the cost of rejected goods was quite high. Cross-functional quality teams were then used to build quality into products right from the start, thereby massively reducing the cost of nonconforming goods.

Total Quality Control

One of the hotbeds of quality concepts is Japan, where *total quality control* (TQC) was developed. It is a broad-ranging set of techniques that are employed to minimize errors throughout an organization. By doing so, a business can greatly improve both its profits and customer satisfaction. It requires the involvement of employees across the organization who are empowered to make changes. This approach involves a number of concepts, which include the following:

- Quality must come first within the organization. Doing so allows a business to gain the loyalty of customers, from which long-term profitability can be achieved.
- The customer's perception of quality is what matters, rather than the producer's perception of quality. This means that the business must actively solicit customer opinions in order to learn about their views on product quality.
- The business must break down its functional silos, so that all employees across the organization work together to enhance quality levels.
- Any actions taken to enhance quality must be based on hard data. This means conducting statistical analyses, from which decisions can be made. Conversely, quality enhancement decisions should never be made based on a data-free opinion. The result will be better decisions.
- Decision-making must be driven down into the organization. Doing so makes full use of the creative potential of the entire work force.

- Cross-functional teams must be used to ensure that quality and cost goals are met. The use of these teams tends to mitigate the negative effects of departmental siloes.

Kaizen is a continuous improvement process that is commonly used within a TQC system. It targets small, incremental enhancements to existing processes, and usually involves a large proportion of the work force. Kaizen is most commonly targeted at production processes but can be applied anywhere within a business. The intent behind making these changes is to improve quality and efficiency levels throughout a firm, focusing on such concepts as work standardization, the elimination of waste, and just-in-time activities. When followed for a long period of time, kaizen can result in significant enhancements to an organization that can strongly bolster its competitive position.

> **Note:** The kaizen concept is focused on improving existing systems, rather than replacing them.

Under a TQC system, employees are expected to engage in two types of quality-related activities. One is process control, where they routinely follow standard operating procedures and investigate all deviations from them. In addition, they may initiate process improvements, where they modify processes in search of better results. When these modifications uncover a process improvement, then standard operating procedures are adjusted to incorporate the improvement.

A side effect of TQC is that the company commits to the full-time employment of a core group of employees. In exchange, those employees are expected to work for the company for their entire careers. With the assurance of life-long employment, employees can settle into the long-term business of improving quality levels. Japanese companies accomplished life-long employment by only making this offer to a portion of the work force, with some work being outsourced and other work being handled during peak demand periods by a part-time work force that was let go after demand declined.

Another side effect of TQC is that manufacturers form tight bonds with a core group of suppliers, sometimes by taking seats on their boards. Doing so allows the manufacturers to demand continual quality improvements from their suppliers, in exchange for which they are offered long-term supply contracts. In many cases, the manufacturers become the sole customers of these suppliers, resulting in decision-making dominance over the affairs of the suppliers.

Many of these concepts appear again in the following section, where we cover a selection of concepts promulgated by William Edwards Deming.

Essentials of Quality Management

The key elements of a system of quality management were derived by William Edwards Deming, a quality consultant. In the following paragraphs, we expand upon several elements of his 14 points for management.

From the perspective of what senior management should do, Demings' key point was to enforce a consistency of purpose throughout the organization, targeted at constantly improving products and processes. This purpose should hold true for many years. Such a high level of consistency can be hard for some managers, who tend to shift among a variety of management fads, looking for one that will deliver quick returns for a minimal investment. Deming realized that quality improvements required consistent attention over many years, while the cumulative effect of many small enhancements gradually resulted in very high quality levels.

Deming realized that the only way to gain the cooperation of the entire workforce in the continual support of quality improvements was to ensure that everyone profited from the arrangement. Examples of this arrangement include training employees to take on different jobs if their original ones are eliminated, as well as committing to keep employees on the payroll over the long term, to the greatest extent possible. It also means that employees must be trained in all quality-related principles, so that they understand what the company is trying to do, and can provide assistance in this effort. Overriding these concepts is the need to work with employees, rather than treating them as a disposable asset. Only by building trust with a well-trained, long-term work force is it possible to develop a quality-focused organization.

A key element of getting employees to work together is to break down departmental silos. This means forming teams from the various departments to work together, as well as to eliminate any incentives for departments to *not* work together (such as paying bonuses for department-specific performance). This can be an especially difficult area in which to make improvements, since some department managers may defend their turf ferociously.

Deming wanted to do away with the inspection stations that were traditionally set up at the end of a production process, weeding out any bad products at that point. Doing so merely caught bad products after they had already been manufactured. He instead wanted companies to focus on the product design and production processes, to ensure that products were created that had no quality issues to begin with. This approach greatly reduced the cost of production, because so few products (if any) would now need to be scrapped or reworked.

One of the best ways to enhance quality is by shifting the focus of the purchasing department toward doing business with a smaller group of suppliers that provide higher-quality goods to the company. This requires a major shift away from purchasing the lowest-cost items, and toward purchasing items with the lowest total long-term cost. In short, the purchasing staff has to be reoriented toward finding suppliers that deliver such high-quality items that they never fail, thereby eliminating warranty claims and customer returns. This view of purchasing calls for the development of long-term relations with suppliers, rather than the previous approach of shifting orders to whichever organization is willing to offer the lowest price.

Deming was not happy with the use of quotas and similar goals. Enforcing quotas gives employees the wrong incentive to deliver goods that may have sub-standard quality. It is better to deliver goods that have the correct quality level, even if the quantity produced is lower than management wants. Instead, employees should focus on improving the product design and production processes, so that all goods produced are of an acceptable quality level. Once this quality level is achieved, process capacity can be increased to produce more goods.

Yet another concern for Deming was the existence of merit ranking systems. These systems tend to pit employees against each other in order to gain comparatively better rankings. Since the enhancement of quality requires company-wide attention to processes, it does no good to emphasize the accomplishments of individuals. Instead, the emphasis should be on what the entire group can accomplish to enhance quality levels.

The preceding areas of emphasis run counter to the principles of the traditional top-down decision-making structure of a hierarchical organization, where senior management sets goals and the rest of the organization obeys. Instead, Demings' 14 points require managers to focus more on pushing decision-making down into the organization, with an emphasis on coaching employees in how to improve quality levels.

Lean Practices

Another quality concept that originated in Japan is lean practices. Lean activities are targeted at the identification and elimination of waste within a business. In essence, anything that does not create value is examined to see if it can be eliminated. A large part of the time and resources consumed within most businesses relates to waste, so lean activities can have a powerful impact on efficiency levels. This can result in substantial cost reductions, as well as faster process cycle times. Shortening cycle times is important, since it allows a business to produce more goods and services from the same production base. In effect, shorter cycle time represents an increase in capacity at minimal cost.

There are several types of waste that can be targeted through a lean practices initiative. They are as follows:

- *Downstream waiting.* Whenever employees in a downstream operation are waiting for work to be completed in an upstream work center, the value of their unused time is a wasted resource.
- *Errors.* Any error that requires rework can impose substantial costs on a business, because the time required to investigate the error and then develop a fix is usually many times longer than the normal processing time for the underlying transaction.
- *Unmet needs.* Any product or process design work that does not meet the needs of a targeted customer is considered a waste.
- *Unnecessary movements.* A business might engage in unnecessary movements, such as shifting inventory to an offsite storage location. These movements can be expensive, and yet do not provide any value to the customer.
- *Unnecessary work.* A business might engage in unnecessary work, such as producing finished goods when there is no immediate purchaser. In these situations, the company is investing in resources that do not yield an immediate payback. For example, the production of goods to stock only results in an

unneeded working capital investment, and also exposes the firm to the risk of write-offs due to obsolete inventory.

Examples of waste include management approvals, product inspections, and the monitoring of whether employees arrive at work on time.

> **Tip:** Something that a customer is not willing to pay for can be considered a wasted resource. Also, something that does not transform a product in some way can also be considered a wasted resource.

The Application of Quality

Quality can be applied throughout an organization, wherever steps are taken that provide services to either internal or external customers. These steps generally fall into three categories, which are:

1. *Quality planning.* This essential first step involves defining who the customer is, what the customer wants, developing the product required by this party, creating the supporting processes, and ensuring that operational personnel are aware of these plans.
2. *Quality control.* This second step is the set of processes used to ensure that the product requirements developed in the planning stage are actually met. It is targeted at spotting differences from the plan and correcting them.
3. *Quality improvement.* This third step involves enhancing quality levels substantially from their current level.

Quality Assurance

Quality assurance refers to the complete set of systems directed at meeting designated customer service standards. These systems include the following:

- Establishing the requirements that are considered necessary to deliver high quality to the customer
- Certifying the performance of suppliers with a rating system
- Testing received goods and materials to ensure that they comply with quality standards
- Ensuring that goods and materials are stored properly to avoid damage
- Verifying the ongoing quality of internal processes, with a feedback loop to correct any issues found
- Examining system output to ensure that quality standards are met

Quality assurance tends to focus on the prevention of quality issues early in the process, rather than merely trying to detect quality problems at the point when goods and services are about to be delivered to the customer. Early prevention reduces costs for the manufacturer, because it avoids the costs that would otherwise have been added to a product after the quality issue first arose.

The Need for Global Optimization

As we just noted, quality must be pursued *throughout* an organization. This must be done with a full knowledge of how all company processes mesh together to produce goods. Without a full knowledge of how a change will flow through this system, it is entirely possible that a quality enhancement targeted at one element of a specific process will actually harm the quality level somewhere else, resulting in an overall degradation of quality for the company as a whole. When these unintended consequences arise, it is essential to investigate them thoroughly, to understand why they occurred. Only then can employees learn from the experience. The accumulation of these learning events over time allows a business to enhance quality levels in a more targeted manner.

Global optimization is especially necessary when the focus of a business is entirely on the customer. In this situation, the management hierarchy must be flattened to the greatest extent possible, so that decision-making authority is concentrated near the customer. In this situation, employees are empowered to use their best judgment when dealing with customer issues. This structure makes it more difficult to operate the traditional siloed department structure, where formal oversight of employees is expected. Instead, the department managers who used to oversee all customer interactions are no longer needed, or only operate as coaches.

> **Note:** The goal of any component of an organization's processes is to optimize the goals of the firm as a whole. This means that it is not necessary for any individual component to optimize its own output; instead, it may be acceptable for any component part to operate at a loss, as long as the outcome is optimization of the *entire* system.

Any business might at first appear to be too complex to be optimized – there are simply too many moving parts to oversee. However, the overall performance of any business is mainly driven by a small number of bottleneck operations. As long as the proper functioning of those bottlenecks are attended to, overall optimization can be achieved. Realistically, most organizations have a very small number of bottlenecks, so most management attention should be focused on them; paying excessive attention to anything other than a bottleneck simply does not impact the overall performance of the business all that much. There are several types of bottlenecks that may impact a business, as noted in the following bullet points:

- *Physical bottleneck.* A machine that has a large amount of work-in-process in queue in front of it is obviously being fully used, and so could be a bottleneck.
- *Paradigm bottleneck.* When employees hold a belief that causes them to act in a certain way, this is called a paradigm bottleneck, and can impact a process to such an extent that the belief is considered a constraint. An example is the belief that the only good workstation is one humming along at 100% of capacity, even though there is not enough demand to justify so much work. The result could be a divergence of resources away from the true bottleneck

(perhaps a machine), resulting in suboptimal use of the actual constrained resource. This item is noted again later as a policy constraint. Another paradigm bottleneck is the overriding belief that costs are to be reduced throughout the business, on the assumption that this will cause an inevitable increase in net profits. In reality, more expenditures must be made if doing so results in better utilization of the bottleneck. This item appears as several policy constraints, such as the freight cost reduction rule, the minimum production run rule, and the overtime rule.

- *Policy bottleneck.* This is a management-imposed guideline for how a process is to be conducted. Unless carefully monitored, these policy bottlenecks can interfere with the orderly flow of work through a business. Policy bottlenecks are difficult to find, since it is necessary to track backwards to them by observing their effects on a business. It may be equally difficult to eliminate such a constraint, since it may have been used by employees for years, and they now consider it inviolate. Here are several examples of policy bottlenecks:

  - *Batch sizing rule.* There may be a policy in place that requires a workstation to first fill up an outbound pallet before it will be shifted to a downstream workstation for additional work. This rule is usually implemented in order to keep from overworking the materials handling staff that operates the forklifts that move the pallets. However, this rule also means that the downstream workstations are alternately starved of incoming parts and then flooded with them, given the surging nature of the inventory flow. This rule can be eliminated by using conveyors between workstations or much smaller transport containers.

  - *Bonus plans.* A company frequently employs a variety of bonus plans in order to incentivize employees to alter their behavior in a certain way. For example, there may be a bonus for not using overtime, which can impact the amount of time worked at a bottleneck operation. Or a bonus might reward employees for an increase in profits, which they achieve by increasing finished goods inventory levels and assigning factory overhead to this additional inventory – effectively manufacturing profits by deferring the recognition of certain expenses. These potentially negative effects must be thought through with care before implementing any bonus plans.

  - *Break rule.* Employees are allowed a specific amount of rest time away from their workstations, during which time the machines remain idle. These rules are routinely included in the demands of unions, which justifiably claim that workers need to periodically stand down from their work. This issue can be ameliorated by using roving teams of replacement workers who take over during breaks, even though this may increase the total cost of labor.

  - *Cost reduction rule.* Costs are to be reduced in all parts of the production process, which can negatively impact the ability of a company to support its constrained resource. Instead, more cash should be spent to ensure that the bottleneck operation is fully supported at all times.

o *Economic lot sizing.* The production scheduling system may employ an economic lot sizing rule, which calculates the economically optimal number of units to produce. The trouble is that this optimization formula typically results in more units than are actually needed right now, so that bottleneck time is wasted producing goods for which there is no immediate need. This rule is similar to the following rule related to the minimum production run. Given the tendency of these formulas to over-produce, they should not be used.

o *Minimum production run.* All production runs must generate a certain minimum number of units, which supposedly justifies the equipment setup cost by spreading this cost over an increased number of units. In reality, a larger production run just robs the next job in line of valuable machine time, and may also create excess inventory that is in danger of obsolescence and consumes company cash.

o *Freight cost reduction rule.* Management may attempt to control costs by not allowing any expenditures for overnight freight deliveries. This may keep parts from entering the queue in front of the bottleneck operation in a timely manner, which reduces constraint utilization. While overnight deliveries may be indicative of other problems, they should still be allowed when the materials are needed.

o *Overtime rule.* Overtime may not be allowed, in which case there is no one to operate the bottleneck operation after regular work hours or during breaks, which halts production. On the contrary, overtime should always be allowed at the bottleneck, to ensure the highest possible level of utilization.

o *Production line balance rule.* The industrial engineering staff attempts to convert the production process into a production line, where capacity levels are just enough in all areas to match production requirements. This policy falls apart when there is a production snafu, which reduces the input to the constrained resource and causes total throughput[1] from the entire process to decline.

o *Resource maximization rule.* All phases of the production facility are to be operated at their maximum capacity levels, which results in excess amounts of inventory being generated, which in turn clogs the production floor. Instead, all workstations should operate at whatever level is needed to support the constrained resource, and no more.

• *Raw material bottleneck.* When there is not enough of a raw material available to meet all customer orders, the raw material is the bottleneck. This constraint is most likely to arise when there is excessive industry-wide demand for a

---

[1] Throughput is the number of units that pass through a process over a period of time.

particular raw material, and where there are not enough substitutes available to replace the raw material. In essence, this means that the bottleneck is located at a supplier. Since the supplier is not (usually) under the control of the company, this is one of the more difficult bottlenecks to resolve or manage on an ongoing basis.

- *Sales department bottleneck.* When the sales process is complex, any step in the process that does not have sufficient resources can result in a reduced level of sales. For example, a shortage in sales engineers can result in too few product demonstrations, and therefore in too few sales being completed.

Given the extensive coverage given to policy bottlenecks in the preceding bullet points, it should be evident that global optimization will likely require attention to the negative impacts of policies.

Once any bottleneck has been identified, management attention should be focused entirely on it, to see if there are ways to minimize its negative effects. For example, a third shift might be assigned to a low-capacity machine, or a maintenance team might be assigned to it to ensure that maintenance downtime is minimized. All other activities are less important than the proper management of this bottleneck.

Note: The amount of bottleneck time is fixed, so do not waste this time by running low-quality parts through the operation. These items will eventually be rejected somewhere downstream for being out of specification, so the related amount of bottleneck time will be lost. To mitigate this loss, set up a quality inspection station immediately in front of the bottleneck operation. An additional role is to be proactive in discussing any quality issues found with the operators of upstream workstations, so that flaws are dealt with promptly.

See the author's *Constraint Management* book for more information about how to deal with bottleneck operations.

Meeting Customer Expectations

A key element of quality management is ensuring that customers receive what they expect. If any element of their baseline expectations is not met, they will consider the delivered product to be low quality. For example, if the expectation is that a laptop computer will remain operational during all video calls, and instead it drops these calls every few minutes, then the computer will be considered low quality, even if all of its other operating characteristics are superior. Thus, a business must have a firm knowledge of customer expectations when designing both products and the entire process by which those products are delivered to customers.

In addition to this baseline quality level, a business can also provide customers with unexpected quality elements, such as a car that provides floor lighting along its sides when someone exits the vehicle. Customers can find these unexpected elements to be quite exciting, perhaps to the extent that they become highly loyal to a particular brand. Some organizations spend large sums to innovate continually, always looking for "new and improved' quality elements that will delight their customers.

> **Tip:** A good source of information regarding customer perceptions of product and process quality is the customer service department. These people communicate with customers all the time, and so are in the best position to understand quality issues. Given the importance of the customer service group in providing this information, it should be given a relatively high status within the organization.

Over time, what were once considered to be unexpected quality elements will be considered standard expectations, so businesses must continually improve their products and processes to keep up with expectations. For example, the original expectation for televisions was a black and white screen, which was supplanted by a color screen, after which remote controls, larger televisions, and smart televisions became the norm. Any manufacturer still producing just black and white televisions would have a hard time selling a single unit, since customer expectations have advanced so far past that point.

If management decides to sell modified products to a variety of product niches, then it should be aware that customer perceptions of quality may vary, depending on the niche. For example, customers in the German market might be accustomed to more rapid product delivery of a vacuum cleaner than was the case in the seller's home market, while customers in the Indian market want a stripped-down version at a lower price point, and customers in the United States prefer to have it delivered with several attachments for different cleaning purposes. Thus, it is essential to understand the baseline quality requirements in each targeted niche, and ensure that they are met.

The Importance of Customer Service

Since the customer service department is in the best position to hear about quality issues from customers, it makes sense to give these employees a great deal of latitude in settling customer issues. To do so, customer service personnel must be given detailed training in how to remediate customer issues, so that they will know what concerns can be settled on the spot and which ones must be referred to someone else in the organization. This training also shows them how to decide upon the size of monetary commitment that the company will make, such as replacing products or just having them sent back for free-of-charge repairs. This training should be ongoing, so that employees are aware of new issues as they arise, and understand how to deal with them. Furthermore, training should encompass how the decisions made within the customer service department impact other parts of the business. For example, granting a free repair to a customer means that the receiving department needs to be prepared to receive the goods, while the repairs department may need to obtain replacement parts in advance of the product's arrival.

Another way to enhance the effectiveness of the department is to screen new customer service candidates to ensure that they have the right personalities for dealing with customers. This means focusing during the selection process on whether candidates have sufficient pools of patience, positive behaviors, and judgment to have successful customer service careers. Conversely, all candidates who are apt to argue or become defensive are screened out of the selection process. This may call for the use of psychological tests and role playing to determine which people should advance through the selection process.

> **Tip:** Customers who have had their complaints promptly and courteously dealt with are more likely to make repeat purchases than someone who never lodged a complaint at all, so an effective customer service function can actually *increase* sales.

The customer service staff should log all complaints received, so that these problems can be delved into to find underlying problems requiring remediation. Such aggregation is especially useful for determining whether there are any particular areas in which complaints are concentrated, so that analysts can dig deeper in these areas to spot quality problems. A likely outcome of this reporting is that analysts will be targeted at those problems that are most damaging to customer relations (such as products that are dead on arrival); all other reported problems are assigned a lower priority, and will be addressed after the most important items have been dealt with.

> **Tip:** Have the customer service staff proactively contact the 20% of all customers that are responsible for 80% of all sales (the Pareto Principle), to see if they are experiencing any issues. This is a useful activity, because any unresolved quality issues among these customers can have a seriously negative impact on sales. At a more advanced level, this may result in the creation of a formal relationship management program.

The Cost of Quality

The cost of quality is the accumulated cost of not creating a quality product. In other words, the cost of quality is any cost that would not have been incurred if a product were perfect. These costs can include reworking a product, testing it, field service to make corrections after a product has been installed, and replacing a faulty product. This aggregate cost is reported to management to give them a basis for ensuring that processes always produce to customer expectations. This information is especially useful for deciding where to invest funds to improve quality levels, so that the return on investment is maximized.

A customer perceives a product as having a high level of quality if it conforms to his expectations. Thus, high quality is really just making sure that a product does what a customer expects it to do. This view of quality means that a company can eliminate any costs that customers have no quality perceptions about. The cost reduction can impact a great many areas. For example, it may be perfectly acceptable to use lower-quality or thinner materials, or to allow blemishes in areas where customers cannot see them, or to allow production at a lower tolerance level than is currently the case (which eliminates some rework costs). There are several types of costs that are impacted by the quality of a product, as noted below:

- *Preventive costs*. These are costs incurred to avoid product failures. These costs include production procedure development, staff training, product design reviews, product testing, preventive maintenance on the machinery used to create products, and supplier qualification assessments.
- *Appraisal costs*. These are the costs of inspection needed to reduce the risk of sending defective products to customers. These costs include supplier component testing, quality control product testing, process analysis, laboratory support, and the cost of any testing equipment.
- *Internal failure costs*. These are the costs associated with defective products that are uncovered prior to delivery to customers. These costs include rework of the defective products, rework caused by design changes, additional testing of the reworked products, scrap, purchasing replacement parts, and the lost profit on products that must be sold as seconds.
- *External failure costs*. These are the costs associated with defective products that are uncovered subsequent to delivery to customers. These costs include lost revenue from customers who will not buy from the company again, the processing of returned goods, administering warranty claims, field service costs, liability lawsuits, and possibly even a comprehensive product recall.

It is more cost-effective to pay for cost improvements in-house, rather than waiting for customers to discover defects. The primary reason is that customers are much less likely to buy from the company again if they discover defects, which can make external failure costs more expensive than all other costs combined.

Modern accounting systems are not designed to compile information about the cost of quality, and so managers have no idea how serious the problem can be. Studies of the cost of quality have generated wildly varying amounts, ranging from five percent of sales all the way up to 30 percent of sales. No matter where the actual amount may lie within this range, the potential cost savings are enormous – among the highest that can be achieved from any management initiative. Consequently, it can make sense to develop cost collection systems that are targeted at quality issues. When doing so, a key concern is balancing the cost of the data collection against the value of the data obtained. Also, unmeasured quality costs are more likely to increase, so cost collection systems need to be installed where this situation is most likely to arise.

Tip: Data collection for the cost of quality does not have to be overly precise. If rough cost estimates can be derived that reveal the general nature of certain costs (such as lost revenue from customers and liability lawsuits), this should be sufficient for decision-making purposes, and may also be relatively inexpensive. Also, such estimates could be derived annually at modest cost, rather than through the creation of an ongoing data collection system.

Note: In addition to managing based on the cost of quality, it is also essential to develop goods and services that delight customers. Otherwise, a business could work its quality costs down to zero, and yet generate minimal sales and profits.

As a general rule, the more expensive internal and external failure costs can be reduced by investing more in the up-front costs of prevention and appraisal. This means that there is an optimum point at which the amounts of all four types of costs can be optimized – usually by incurring the bulk of all quality costs in the areas of prevention and appraisal. A business could attempt to increase its quality level past this optimum point, but doing so would result in a higher-than-optimal total cost of quality.

The Cost of Conformance

The cost of conformance includes all expenses incurred to ensure that a product meets the minimum quality standard. Conformance costs include standards application, employee training, process documentation, product inspections, and product testing. When incurring these costs, the intent is to avoid product failures.

The cost of conformance is usually much less than the costs that a business would otherwise incur, such as the cost of a product recall due to product failures in the marketplace. Therefore, it makes sense to invest in detecting instances of nonconformance as soon after they occur as possible. After that point, additional costs will be incurred that will be lost once the nonconformance is eventually detected. For example, a faulty part is created at a work station, after which it is included in a completed product and shipped to the customer, where it fails and needs to be sent back to the company for replacement. All of these subsequent costs would have been avoided if the fault had been discovered as soon as the part was produced.

> **Tip:** Early detection of nonconformance makes it more likely that the cause of the nonconformance can be immediately spotted and corrected. This is not the case when a nonconformance is detected by a customer, since it may now be too late to research the underlying issue.

The Cost of Nonconformance

The cost of nonconformance is comprised of those costs incurred as the result of a failure to meet the quality standards for a product. These costs are triggered when problems in the production process cause imperfections that render products unusable. The costs can include rework, scrap, field service costs, warranty replacements, and the cost of lost customers.

Reporting on the Cost of Quality

It is cost-prohibitive to create a cost of quality tracking system that is absolutely comprehensive. Such a system would require a massive amount of data collection, and may very well offset any benefits to be gained from the system. Instead, eliminate any costs that are inordinately difficult to measure, assess what the resources are for measuring the remaining costs, and finally discuss with management which specific types of quality-related costs they wish to monitor. The result will likely be a cost collection system that varies over time, redirecting its focus to different costs as management gradually tackles and improves upon each one.

One way to aggregate cost of quality information is to create new accounts for them in the chart of accounts. However, it may be difficult for the accounting staff to discern which costs to assign to these accounts, so in many cases it may make more sense to track the costs on a project basis only; by doing so, one can undertake a small collection effort and store the information in an electronic spreadsheet. Afterwards, if the results of the project indicate that there can be long-term cost reductions to be gained from continual cost collection efforts, it may be worth investigating the use of general ledger accounts in which to store this information.

Once the cost of quality information has been collected, format it into a report structure that presents the maximum amount of actionable information to management. The following example uses a format that aggregates costs into the four types of quality costs already described – prevention, appraisal, internal failure, and external failure. This format not only shows management where most of its quality costs lie (clearly in the external failure cost area), but also the sub-categories of expenses from which these costs are originating. This report format tells management roughly where to look if it wants to reduce its cost of quality.

EXAMPLE

The president of Rapunzel Hair Products commissions a cost of quality analysis to determine where the company incurred the bulk of its quality-related costs over the past three-month period. Her intent is to use the results of this study to focus more closely on reducing costs in the areas where most costs are incurred. The results are:

Cost Type / Cost Line Item	Cost Line Item Results	Summary Totals
Prevention Cost Category		
Production procedure development	$6,500	
Staff training	5,000	
Product testing	2,000	
Preventive maintenance	12,000	
Supplier qualification assessments	19,000	
		$44,500
Appraisal Cost Category		
Supplier component testing	$4,200	
Quality control product testing	5,000	
Process analysis	7,100	
Testing equipment	3,000	
		$19,300

Cost Type / Cost Line Item	Cost Line Item Results	Summary Totals
Internal Failure Cost Category		
Rework of defective products	$23,000	
Testing of reworked products	3,800	
Purchasing replacement parts	1,900	
Lost profit on products sold as seconds	25,000	
		$53,700
External Failure Cost Category		
Processing of returned goods	$61,000	
Administering warranty claims	23,000	
Field service costs	5,900	
		$89,900
Total		$207,400

The report reveals that internal and external failure costs comprise 69% of the company's $207,400 total cost of quality, with the processing of returned goods being by far the largest cost incurred.

This report can also be converted into a percentage of sales format, which is useful if sales are varying a great deal over the reporting timeline. The cost of quality varies with sales volume, so if sales are fluctuating, only a percentage of sales format will show if a cost of quality reduction campaign is really working.

The preceding cost of quality report tells management what types of general quality costs a company is incurring, but it does nothing to inform them about where specific quality problems are arising. Locating such information requires detailed investigative work. It may be necessary to conduct a separate root cause analysis for each problem encountered, such as the one in the following example. This report tells management what is causing a quality cost and the proportion of total incidents. They use this report to take immediate action steps. Thus, the report in the preceding example is needed to give them a general view of where quality costs occur, and the root cause analysis to create a cost reduction action.

EXAMPLE

The president of Rapunzel Hair Products reviews the cost of quality report and decides that the rework of defective products (which costs $23,000) is the most troubling. She asks an operations analyst to delve further into this specific area, and create a root cause analysis report.

He investigates the situation, targeting the reasons why products become defective. He finds that there is roughly a 50/50 split between problems arising from purchased goods and from goods manufactured in Rapunzel's own facilities. From this analysis, he investigates further and then generates the following report:

Proportion of Incidents	Root Cause	Recommendation
Purchased Goods Issues		
39%	Performance specifications were incorrect	Tighten the tolerances on purchased product specifications (may result in cost increase)
32%	Damaged in Rapunzel warehouse	Change putaway and picking procedures. Also require suppliers to ship in more robust packaging
18%	Supplier quality too low	Institute supplier certification system and prepare to change suppliers
11%	Other issues not investigated	
100%		
Manufactured Goods Issues		
41%	Inferior quality raw materials	Purchase higher grade resin (may result in cost increase)
29%	Scratches incurred during internal moves	Replace move containers with padded versions
13%	Machine tolerances incorrect	Revise machine setup procedures
17%	Other issues not investigated	
100%		

The report indicates that there will be a cost associated with several of the proposed fixes, which will require a management decision. Another major cause of problems is the packaging and handling of products, which will likely require further analysis to determine precise causes.

The preceding report gives management detailed information that it can act on, or which at least takes it well down the path of finding the root cause of a quality problem.

Product Audits

A business may want to conduct a product audit, to discern the quality level that customers experience when using a product. This audit has a broader scope than a simple product inspection, since it is also designed to provide ideas for product improvement, while also reviewing the quality being produced by the system. Product audits are frequently conducted based on products purchased in the marketplace, rather than using finished goods from the warehouse. Doing so introduces any damage caused by shipping and storage activities.

A product audit focuses on the quality levels experienced by customers. This means documenting both major and minor discrepancies that would be noted by a customer. The following exhibit shows a summary of a product audit results for a new car, drawn from a sample of 100 cars.

New Car Audit Results

Issue Found	Seriousness	Weighting	Frequency
Door dings	Minor	1	8
Bumper scratches	Minor	1	12
Does not start	Critical	5	2
Trim out of alignment	Minor	1	7
Windshield cracked	Minor	1	4

When deciding which issues to examine as part of a product audit, you should develop a hierarchy of importance for product characteristics. Doing so focuses attention on those characteristics that are of most importance to the customer. The usual classifications are critical, major, and minor. A critical characteristic is any product feature that presents a safety hazard or which can cause a severely negative impact to the company's reputation in the marketplace. A major characteristic is any feature other than a critical one that would result in reduced product usability if it were to fail. A minor characteristic is one that would be noticed by customers, but which does not fall into the critical or major classifications.

Summary

In this chapter, we have emphasized the extraordinary extent to which quality impacts the success of a business. If it produces products that meet customer expectations – without deficiencies - then it will succeed. If not, then it will incur costs throughout the organization that will have a severe impact on its profitability. Consequently, it is essential to make management aware of both the costs and benefits of quality, and how changes can be made throughout the organization to take advantage of this key concept.

Chapter 2
Process Control

Introduction

Process control involves the collection of data about a process, from which out-of-control situations can be detected. If these situations are found, the party responsible for the process makes changes to bring the process back into control. In this chapter, we cover the various techniques used to spot variances from expectations within a process.

Sampling Systems

Acceptance sampling is used to determine the quality of a batch of products. It involves picking a representative number of units for testing from the batch. The quality of the selected units is then viewed as being representative of the quality level of the entire batch. The basic steps involved in acceptance testing are as follows:

1. Determine the size of the batch to be tested.
2. Determine the number of units to be sampled.
3. Determine the number of defects considered to be acceptable.
4. If the number of defects found is below the acceptable threshold, then accept the batch. If not, then reject it.
5. Determine the remedial action to be taken in the event of a batch rejection, such as scrapping, rework, or returning parts to suppliers.
6. Determine what corrective action should be taken in the event of a batch rejection, such as shutting down the process or switching to 100% inspection.

Acceptance testing is used in situations where a business cannot test every one of its products. This is the case when it is not cost-effective to test every unit, or to do so within a reasonable period of time. Acceptance testing may also be needed when a thorough test could damage a product or make it unfit for sale.

The problem with acceptance sampling is that it assumes the underlying population is homogeneous, and that the samples have been drawn from a stable process – which is not necessarily the case. Consequently, it is almost always better to use a p-chart. A *p-chart* is an attributes control chart used with data collected from batches of varying sizes. Because the batch size can vary, a p-chart shows the proportion of non-conforming items, rather than the actual count. The process attribute is described in a yes/no, pass/fail, or go/no go form. For example, you could use a p-chart to plot the proportion of incorrectly assembled products each week. The batch size would vary, depending on the total number of products produced. P-charts are extremely useful for determining whether a process is stable and predictable. A sample p-chart appears in the following exhibit.

Sample P-Chart

Day Number	Units Examined	Defective Units	Fraction Defective
1	100	22	0.22
2	100	33	0.33
3	100	24	0.24
4	100	20	0.20
5	100	18	0.18
6	100	24	0.24
7	100	24	0.24
8	100	29	0.29
9	100	18	0.18
10	100	27	0.27
11	100	31	0.31
12	100	26	0.26
13	100	31	0.31
14	100	24	0.24
15	100	22	0.22
16	100	22	0.22
17	100	29	0.29
18	100	31	0.31
19	100	21	0.21
20	100	26	0.26
21	100	24	0.24
22	100	32	0.32
23	100	17	0.17
24	100	25	0.25
25	100	21	0.21

When using a p-chart, the decision for whether to ship a product to customers is as follows:

$$\text{If } p < (K_1 \div K_2) \text{ then ship}$$

Where:

K_1 = The cost to inspect one unit
K_2 = Cost of shipping a defective unit

For example, if the cost to inspect a unit is $2 and the cost of shipping a defective unit is $100 (given the loss of customer goodwill), then process output with an average defective outcome fraction of less than 2% could be shipped without engaging in any additional inspection work.

Another variation is to test 100% of all units when it is critical for all units to operate within planned specifications. This draconian level of testing is also required when a process is out of control, since there is no way to be reliably assured that any untested units are not defective.

In the preceding cases, we have to accept that there is a given amount of variability within a batch of produced units. This variability may come from a large array of causes, not all of which are known. Whether a unit is considered to have been accepted or not depends on whether it varies within a given set of parameters. If the parameters are set close together, then more units will likely be considered to be defective. Conversely, looser parameters will result in fewer units being considered defective, since there is more allowed variability in the outcome. In either case, you are accepting that there will be a certain amount of variation in the outcome.

Note: A critical point when dealing with process variation is that these variations are largely outside of the control of production workers. This is because few production workers are involved in the design of the process of which they are a part, and so have no control over it. Therefore, it makes little sense to chastise or reward workers for the output that they produce.

Control Charts

A *control chart* is a statistical control used to analyze process variables and monitor their effects on performance. A control chart states upper and lower control limits, which are thresholds used to detect out-of-control outcomes. The centerline of the chart is the average finding for the process being tracked.

If the plotted data points are all within the control limits, then a process is considered to be in control. If some data points fall outside of the control limits, then the process is considered to be out of control. The upper and lower control limits are set at the highest and lowest (respectively) values that would be impacted by common causes of variation. A visual examination of a control chart reveals whether defects are occurring randomly or systematically; in the latter case, corrective action is required.

Tip: Consider collecting data for small groups of units, since doing so may uncover process shifts more frequently than would have been the case for a large number of units where these shifts may be lost in the data. This is especially useful when initially examining a new process for which there is minimal data about the issues that trigger variances.

When there is a good reason for reducing process variation, then it can make sense to retain the control charts for prior periods, so that the additional data can be used to tease out possible causes of variations. For example, control charts could be run for specific machine operators, specific machines, or specific raw materials – each of which might be triggering a variation.

EXAMPLE

The Christmas Candy Cane Factory manufactures candy canes. A problem has been detected in the production line, for which a project team is created to find a solution. The team finds that the normal processing time to combine white and red batches of candy, twist and stretch the batch, clip off individual candy canes and bend them into an arc is 10 minutes. There are modest variations in this time period that are caused by operator expertise. A sample control chart for the process follows.

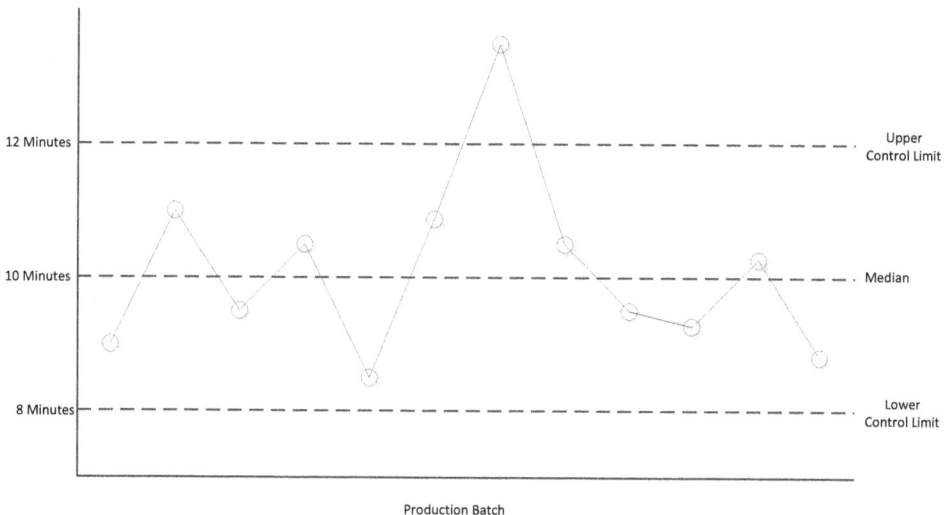

In the chart, there is one massive spike in the data. This was caused by an incorrect batch formulation that softened the candy cane batch, requiring extra processing time to let the batch cure. If management wants to act on this variation, it can set up a procedure in the batch formulation process to ensure that the correct ingredients are used.

When there is a one-time spike in the data (such as in the preceding exhibit), it makes sense to collect data more frequently, so that the cause of the spike can be more readily determined. Conversely, if data collection only occurs at long intervals, it becomes much more difficult to ascertain the cause of a spike.

A common finding when control charts are used is trend patterns, where you can see that a series of measurements are pointing toward an out-of-condition event. These trends point toward looming mechanical problems, such as a machine beginning to wear out or which is in need of adjustment. The following control chart shows such a trend, where the pattern is clearly visible well before a measurement actually breaches the upper control limit.

Sample Control Chart with Trending Data

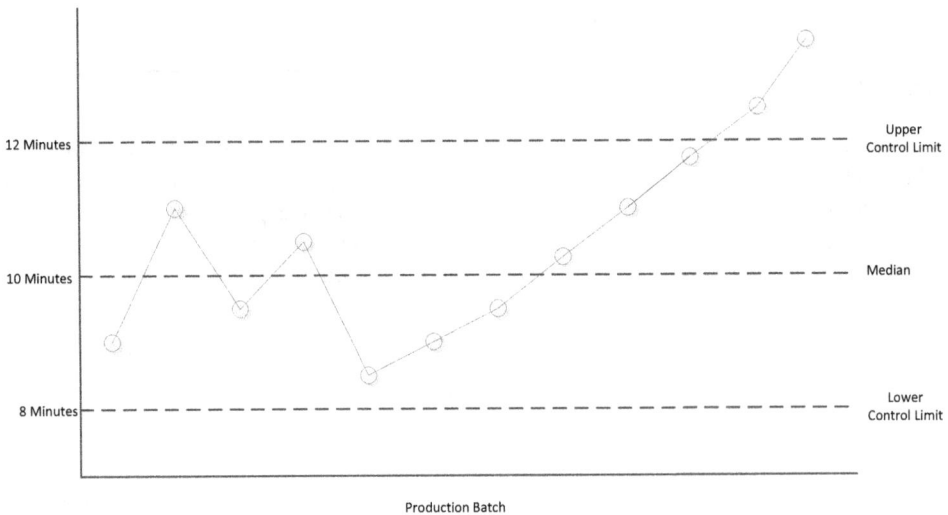

The arrival of an upward or downward-sloping trend line in the data likely indicates the presence of a special cause of variation that needs to be investigated and corrected. Otherwise, this special cause will eventually result in process variations that are outside of the upper or lower control limits.

Data Analysis

In quality management, a constant issue is being able to collect data, organize it, and draw meaningful conclusions from it. This analysis frequently involves finding the midpoint of the data, as well as the spread of the data around that midpoint. In this section, we discuss how to extract insights from data.

Frequency Distribution

A *frequency distribution* is a data set that is organized to show the frequency of occurrence of each possible outcome of a repeatable event. In short, it reveals how frequently a particular value occurs. For example, the frequency distribution for a pizza shop is 10 pizzas during the 5-6 p.m. time slot, 30 pizzas during the 6-7 p.m. slot, 16 pizzas during the 7-8 p.m. slot, and 12 pizzas during the 8-9 p.m. slot. To obtain a frequency distribution, you have to sort the data set and count how many of each value you have. A sample of how a frequency distribution can be used appears in the following exhibit, where a business is tracking the number of inventory record keeping issues found during one week of cycle counts. The analysis is sorted in declining order of frequency, so that management's attention is drawn to the highest-frequency problems first.

Frequency Distribution for Inventory Record Keeping Issues Found

	Day					
	Mon.	Tue.	Wed.	Thu.	Fri.	Total
Incorrect unit of measure	||	||||				|||||	12
Incorrect quantity		||	||||			|||	10
Incorrect part number	|||				|||||		9
Incorrect bin location					|||		||	7
Total	6	8	7	7	10	38

The Mean, Median, and Mode

Data analysis frequently involves finding the midpoint of the data, and then determining the spread of the data around that midpoint. The midpoint can be described in three ways – the mean, median, and mode.

The *mean* is the average of a group of numbers. To calculate it, add up the numbers and divide by how many numbers are in the group. For example, the mean of the following group of numbers is calculated as follows:

$$2, 8, 15, 21, 41, 41, 52$$

$$2 + 8 + 15 + 21 + 41 + 41 + 52 = 180$$

$$180 \div 7 \text{ numbers} = \mathbf{26}[2]$$

The *median* is the amount of the middle number in a sorted list of numbers, so that half the data in the sample are above the median and half are below it. The median represents the approximate average amount of a set of numbers, though the individual values in the set can skew the median higher or lower than the actual average. The following steps are used to derive the median:

1. Sort the list of numbers in ascending order.
2. If the number of values is an odd number, the middle figure in the list is the median.
3. If the number of values is an even number, the average of the middle pair of numbers is the median.

For example, the median is the fourth number (stated in bold) in the following sorted list of numbers, where there are three numbers on either side of this value:

$$2, 8, 15, \mathbf{21}, 41, 41, 52$$

---

[2] The number is rounded. The actual value is approximately 25.71.

The *mode* is the cluster of numbers in a group of numbers that occurs most frequently. In the list of numbers that we have been using, the only number that appears twice is 41, so that is the mode for that group of numbers.

Of the three calculation methods, the most accurate of the group was the mean, since it represented the average of all values. The median value skewed low, since there was no value in the group that was more representative of the middle value of the group. The mode was the least accurate, because the only numerical duplication in the group was well out on the higher end of the values in the group. The mode will not always be so far away from the numerical average; when the values in a group are tightly clustered together, the mode may be quite close to the numerical average.

Standard Deviation

Standard deviation is a measure of the amount of variation or dispersion of a set of values. A low standard deviation indicates that the values tend to be close to the mean of a group of numbers, while a high standard deviation indicates that the values are spread out over a wider area. For example, a company might want to test the ability of its production process to manufacture goods that are within the specifications demanded by its customers. If the standard deviations of its quality assurance tests are tightly clustered, then the production process is working as intended. The standard deviation formula is as follows:

$$\sqrt{\frac{\sum x^2 - n(m)^2}{n-1}}$$

Where:

$\sum x^2$ = Each value from the population, squared and then summed
m = The population mean
n = The size of the population

As an example of how the standard deviation calculation works, we have three lists of numbers, all of which have a mean average of 10. They are as follows:

Data set #1: 2,4,6,8,10,10,10,10,10,10,10,10,10,10,10,10,10,10,10,12,14,16,18

Data set #2: 2,4,4,6,6,6,8,8,8,8,10,10,10,12,12,12,12,14,14,14,16,16,18

Data set #3: 2,2,2,2,2,2,2,2,2,2,2,10,18,18,18,18,18,18,18,18,18,18,18

It is not efficient to manually run the standard deviation calculation for these data sets. Instead, we will enter the data into Excel and let it do the calculation work for us. In the following exhibit, we have posted data set #1 in column A, data set #2 in column

B, and data set #3 in column C, with the standard deviation outcome shown at the bottom of each column. The Excel formula used for this calculation is as follows:

$$=STDEV.S(A3:A25)$$

This formula runs the calculation for the data set loaded into cells A3 through A25.

In the exhibit, note the large differences in standard deviation that appear in row 27. This is because the numbers are more tightly clustered around the mean in the first data set, and are progressively more dispersed in the next two data sets.

Standard Deviation Calculation in Excel

	A	B	C
1	Data	Data	Data
2	Set #1	Set #2	Set #3
3	2	2	2
4	4	4	2
5	6	4	2
6	8	6	2
7	10	6	2
8	10	6	2
9	10	8	2
10	10	8	2
11	10	8	2
12	10	8	2
13	10	10	2
14	10	10	10
15	10	10	18
16	10	12	18
17	10	12	18
18	10	12	18
19	10	12	18
20	10	14	18
21	10	14	18
22	12	14	18
23	14	16	18
24	16	16	18
25	18	18	18
26			
27	3.303	4.264	8.000

Standard deviations can be incorporated into control charts. Doing so can be quite effective in spotting significant deviations from the midpoint of the data.

Variance Analysis

A *variance* is the difference between an expected value and an actual value, stated as either an actual number or a percentage. Variances are typically derived from a budgeted baseline. For example, a variance can describe a change in unit values, such as the difference between the recorded number of units in stock and the actual number of units on hand, as per a physical count.

It is generally best to measure variances as a percentage of the baseline value, in order to gain a better sense of the impact of the variance. For example, an inventory variance of $50,000 might initially appear to be significant, until you realize that the baseline inventory figure from which it was derived is $1 billion – in which case the variance is immaterial. Conversely, a $50,000 variance that arises when the total amount expected to be spent is only $10,000 is certainly worth investigating.

To calculate a variance, subtract the actual amount from the baseline value. The resulting variance will be classified as negative if the actual value is larger than the baseline, while the variance will be positive if the actual value is smaller than the baseline.

Summary

The analysis techniques described in this chapter are useful for spotting out-of-control situations. The most efficient way to bring these processes back under control is to prepare out-of-control action plans that state the actions to be taken once a problematic situation is detected. These plans work best when they are accompanied by a visual action statement, such as a flowchart, that provides an easy view of how to take the required steps.

Chapter 3
Quality Management Tools

Introduction

Thus far, we have provided an overview of quality management and process control, without addressing the tools that are available for identifying and correcting specific problem areas. A representative sampling of these tools appears in this chapter.

Business Process Diagrams

A *business process diagram* (BPD) graphically depicts the flow of business processes. The intent is to generate a simplified, easy-to-understand overview of a process, which can then be used to identify problem areas. A minimal number of symbols are used in a BPD, usually just a rectangle to describe activities and arrows to indicate the flow of activities. A sample BPD for the purchase of goods appears in the following example.

When preparing a BPD, consider using the following best practices to generate higher-quality diagrams:

- *Standardize the flow.* The information in a BPD should begin at the top or in the top left corner and proceed to the bottom or bottom right corner, thereby establishing a standard flow.
- *Minimize information.* Ideally, a BPD should contain much less information than a narrative description of a system, so that only the highlights of the basic process steps are revealed.
- *Eliminate insignificant items.* Strip out minor steps that are rarely used. It makes more sense to focus on those aspects of the system that are used on a repetitive basis.
- *Terminate the BPD.* If any activities or documents continue off the bottom of the BPD, identify the name of the chart in which the description continues. Otherwise, the reader does not gain a complete understanding of the underlying process.
- *Conduct a walkthrough.* Conduct a joint walkthrough of the BPD with someone else who is knowledgeable in the targeted system, to see if there are any errors or omissions that need to be corrected.
- *Simplify the format.* Since this is a high-level diagram, simplify it as much as possible by only using two columns. The first column states who is engaged in an activity, while the second column describes their activities.
- *Stay high level.* A BPD is constructed at such a high level that there is no need to delve into the details of exactly which documents are used, or which

software is employed to process data. This means that a BPD is much less likely to require revision as certain aspects of a system are altered over time.

Purchasing Business Process Diagram

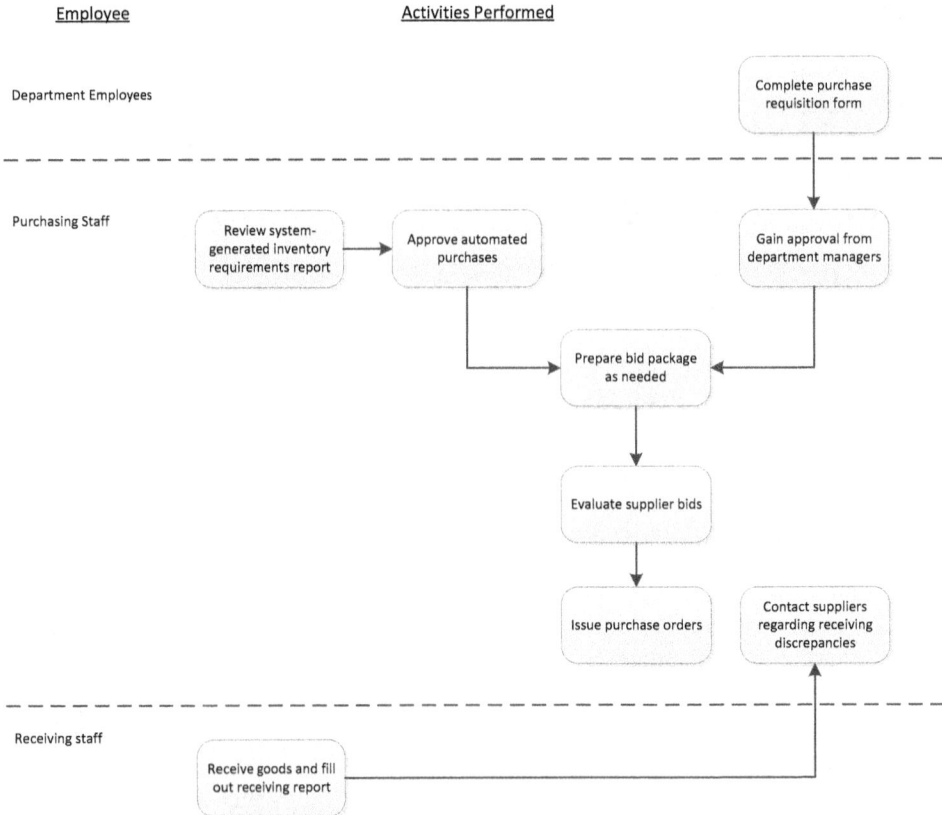

Employee   Activities Performed

Department Employees

Complete purchase requisition form

Purchasing Staff

Review system-generated inventory requirements report

Approve automated purchases

Gain approval from department managers

Prepare bid package as needed

Evaluate supplier bids

Issue purchase orders

Contact suppliers regarding receiving discrepancies

Receiving staff

Receive goods and fill out receiving report

Cause-and-Effect Diagrams

A *cause-and-effect diagram* is a visual layout of the possible causes of a problem. It is structured to show a number of branches, and so looks somewhat like a fish skeleton (hence its alternate name of fishbone diagram). A cause-and-effect diagram begins with a single line, at the end of which is stated the problem to be solved. Then a number of branches are added that denote the general areas in which the causes of problems may be found. The generic headings most commonly used for these problem areas are:

- Methods (procedures)
- Machines (equipment)
- People
- Materials

- Measurement
- Environment

With this basic structure in place, a facilitator then collects possible causes from the team assigned to the problem, and writes them into the diagram. The outcome is a diagram similar to the following sample. This approach does a good job of organizing information about the causes of a problem.

Sample Cause-and-Effect Diagram

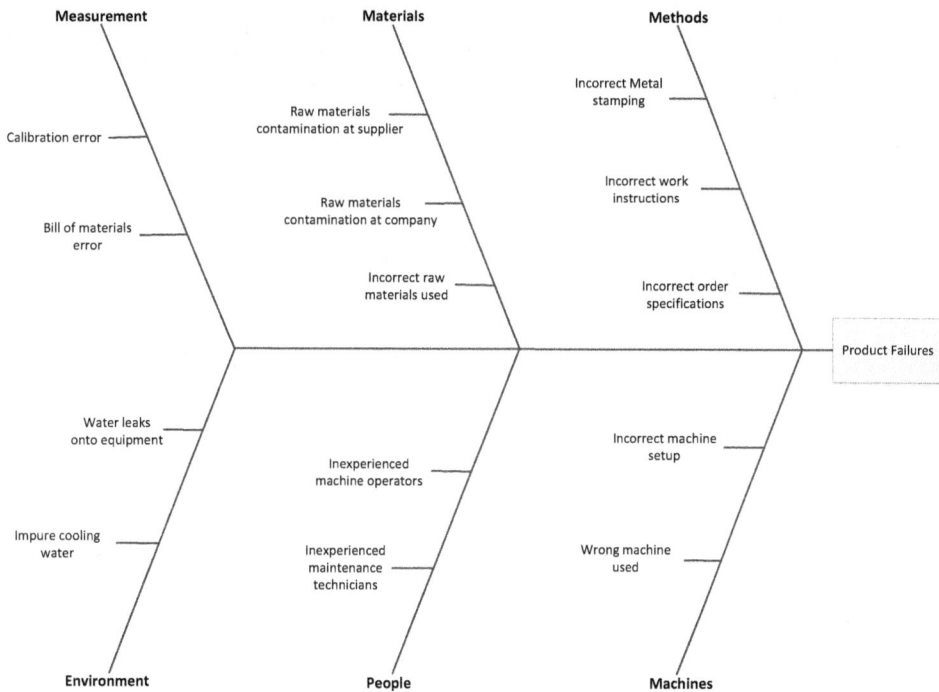

Failure Prevention

Quality failures can be divided into several groups of failure types, of each which calls for a different failure prevention response. The first failure type is the *inadvertent error*, which is due to a lack of attention. For example, a production person with vast experience might mistakenly drill an extra hole in a product through a lack of attention, or an accounting clerk might mistakenly file an invoice in the wrong folder. These types of failures occur all the time, and can represent a significant cost to a business. Inadvertent errors can be eliminated through the use of foolproofing, where processes are designed so that actions can only be completed one way; it is simply not possible to complete an action in any other manner. For example, a part can be designed to only fit into a production machine one way, thereby eliminating the risk of having someone inadvertently install it backwards. Or, the obvious solution to misfiling a document is to not file it at all – instead, the document is scanned and stored electronically, with the system automatically indexing it based on a bar code on the document.

Tip: Any process that is highly repetitive should be automated to the greatest extent possible, since these are the areas in which employees are most likely to be inattentive and make inadvertent errors. The cost of the errors avoided can be considered in justifying the investment in automation.

The second failure type is the *technique error*, where an employee uses an improper technique as part of a process. For example, a production worker might have speeded up a lamination machine because he was bored, resulting in products delaminating. The resolutions are similar to those used for inadvertent errors, such as automation and foolproofing. In addition, remedial training might be used to resolve the issue, as well as better work instructions.

The third failure type is the *willful error*, where someone intentionally causes an error. These errors are difficult to detect, because the party responsible for them is only triggering errors when no one is watching. Also, the errors made typically make no engineering sense from a product or process design perspective, making them more difficult to research. Obviously, these errors are caused by employee disaffection, such as being given notice of termination, or having one's pay cut. It is nearly impossible to spot these issues, since a great deal of ingenuity may go into their commission. Typically, willful error is only considered an option when inadvertent and technique errors have already been considered and discarded.

Pareto Analysis

Pareto analysis is a method of analysis based on the concept that 20% of the variables included in an analysis are responsible for 80% of the results. For example, 20% of all customers are responsible for 80% of all customer service activity, or 20% of all inventory items comprise 80% of the inventory value. Pareto analysis is used to concentrate management attention on those issues having the greatest impact on an organization. It is also called the 80/20 rule.

Pareto charts are bar graphs in which the longest bars are positioned on the left and the shortest to the right. This arrangement tells the viewer which situations depicted by the bars are the most significant. The chart may also contain a cumulative total, which appears as an ascending line across the top of the chart. The vertical axis represents the frequency of occurrence, while the horizontal axis identifies the different types of events being tracked by the bars.

A Pareto chart is used when examining the frequency of problems. It is especially useful when there are many problems to sort through, since it draws attention to the most frequently-occurring issues. For the same reason, it is an excellent mode of communication.

In the following sample Pareto chart, a company is trying to determine the frequency of different types of customer complaints, using as a database the customer complaints received in the past month. The chart begins with the most common issue (broken packaging), and then proceeds through a series of additional complaints that are of declining importance to customers. If a project team wanted to eliminate those issues causing nearly all customer complaints, it should focus its attention on just the first two items (broken packaging and incorrect order fulfillment), since the remaining problems represent a minimal proportion of the total number of customer concerns.

Sample Pareto Chart

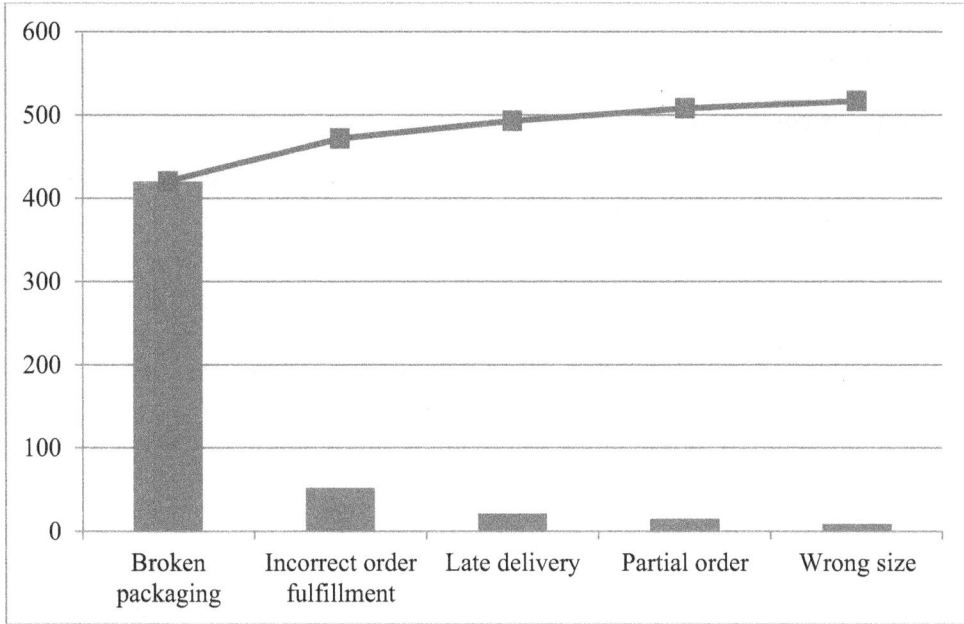

Plan-Do-Check-Act Cycle

The plan-do-check-act cycle describes the process of continuous improvement needed to enact change. It is particularly useful when applied to high-volume processes, since even small changes to these processes can translate into substantial gains for an organization. The cycle involves a series of steps, which are followed iteratively to ensure that change is reinforced over time. The steps are noted below.

Step 1. Plan

Study the current process to determine where it is failing and how it can be improved.

Step 2. Do

Enact change, preferably on a small scale. A small-scale change reduces the amount of investment involved, making the cycle quite cost-effective.

Step 3. Check

Measure the outcome of the implemented change.

Step 4. Act

If the measured result represents an improvement, go ahead and implement the change across the organization. If the check stage resulted in a failure, then go back and try a different improvement plan.

The lessons learned from each iteration of the cycle are incorporated into the next iteration, so that the process improves over time. This approach can result in an ongoing rate of change that is incorporated into a firm's budget as an expected reduction in expenses.

Quality at the Source

Quality at the source means that each employee is held responsible for ensuring the quality of products. This is accomplished with the tools noted below.

- *Mistake proofing.* The intent behind mistake proofing is to delve into the causes of poor quality and correct the underlying issues, so that they do not occur again.
- *Self checks.* Allow workers to measure the specifications of their work, and call for help if units are out of spec.
- *Standardized work.* Use a high level of documentation and training to ensure that each product is manufactured the same way, every time.
- *Successive checks.* Each successive workstation checks the quality of the incoming work. Doing so finds errors in short order, before additional processing work is completed.
- *Visual management.* Use a signaling system to pull engineers and managers to the spot where there is a problem, so that it can be corrected at once.

Root Cause Analysis

Root cause analysis is used to identify the root cause of a problem by asking the question "why" multiple times. This approach is useful for peeling away the layers of symptoms to arrive at the root cause of a problem. By correcting the underlying root causes of problems, the incidence of the problems can be greatly reduced or eliminated. This approach can be used to uncover issues related to the failure of a system, an error by a person, or an organizational issue (such as an incorrect work instruction). The basic process steps to follow in a root cause analysis are as follows:

1. *Define the problem.* State the issue that requires correction, including a specification of the nature, magnitude, timing, and location of events. A high degree of specificity makes it easier to find a root cause.
2. *Obtain evidence.* Collect data pertaining to the problem. The information obtained should relate to every behavior, condition, action, or inaction relating to the problem.

3. *Ask why.* In going through the collected data, inquire into the factors that directly resulted in an effect. This may involve drilling down through a series of "why" questions.

4. *Eliminate causal factors.* A causal factor is an action or inaction that caused an incident or exacerbated an incident. These are simply triggering events and not root causes, and so no action is taken. For example, an employee turns on a laptop computer, which then explodes. Turning on the laptop was not the root cause, but rather something within the device. In short, we must sort through the data and eliminate causal factors, which leave root causes in the data.

5. *Identify corrective actions.* Note those actions that will likely prevent a recurrence of the defined problem.

6. *Identify usable actions.* From the initial set of corrective actions, identify those that are within the control of the business, are cost-effective, and will probably not introduce a new set of problems. When there are several possible actions that meet these criteria, pick the simplest one, since it is easier to implement and maintain.

7. *Implement usable actions.* Obtain the required resources and implement those actions considered usable.

8. *Examine outcome.* Review the process to see if the changes are having a positive impact on the identified problem.

9. *Repeat.* If the problem has not been entirely corrected or at least reduced below a threshold level, repeat the process to identify and implement other usable actions.

It is quite possible that finding and correcting a single root cause will not completely eliminate a particular problem. If so, root cause analysis can be conducted on a recurring basis, to gradually locate and eliminate a series of issues. Eventually, the number of times the triggering problem arises may decline to the point where additional effort is considered unnecessary, though there may be additional root causes still causing problems; the remaining issues are simply considered too immaterial to pursue, or their correction is not cost-effective.

Root cause analysis may require a considerable amount of detailed investigation, not only to find a root cause, but also to generate several possible solutions that will correct the root cause. The solution selected will usually be the simplest or least expensive alternative available, and one that does not trigger a new root cause that leads to a new problem or reinforces an old problem.

Root cause analysis suffers from several problems. A key concern is that project teams tend to find problems that they already suspect. Thus, they tend to select and interpret data that supports their existing opinions, which means that new and unique root causes may not be found. Also, this type of analysis does not identify the severity of a root cause, only the existence of the root cause. When there are several possible root causes, this means that management may choose to spend time and resources eliminating an issue that may prove to have a relatively minor impact on a problem.

Finally, root cause analysis can be quite time-consuming, since it may involve a large amount of data gathering and investigatory work.

Value Stream Mapping

A value stream map (VSM) reveals a considerable amount of information about the activities that we engage in to create value. Depending upon the format used, it can point out such information as:

- The work time and wait time required for each step in a process
- The amount of labor needed for a work step, including the identification of overtime
- The error rate by work step
- Downtime by work step

The resulting charts can be used to pinpoint areas needing improvement, such as reductions in errors, automation to eliminate staff time, and altered controls to shorten process flows.

The VSM concept is best explained with an example. In the following sample of the timekeeping process, we see that the accounting staff requires only a small amount of staffing and time to process two steps, which are issuing reminders to employees and verifying supervisory approval of time cards. However, the VSM indicates that the controller must allocate more staff to the tasks of reviewing received time cards and summarizing hours worked. These latter two tasks are so time-sensitive that they routinely require the use of overtime to be completed on time. The map also shows a high error rate. Further, the VSM reveals that a total of 25.5 hours are needed to complete this step, which is the lengthiest part of the payroll process.

Sample Value Stream Map – Timekeeping

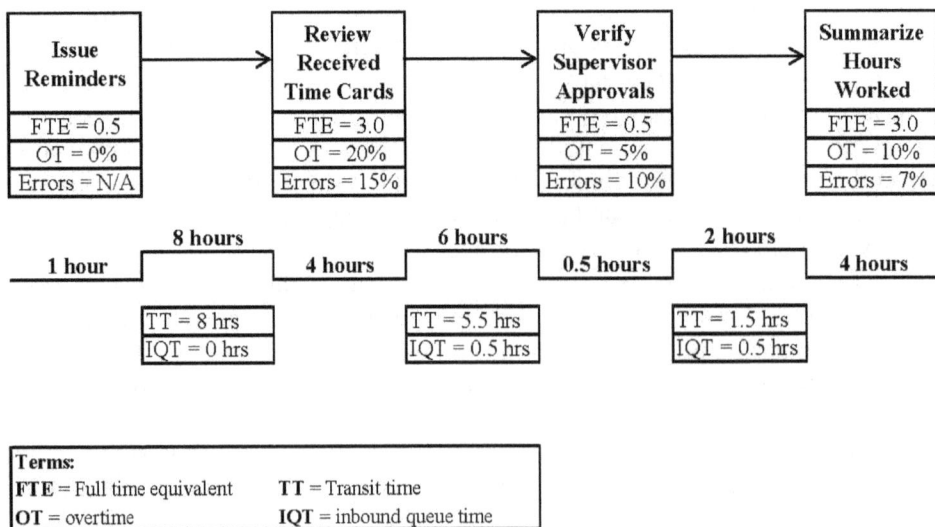

Issue Reminders		Review Received Time Cards		Verify Supervisor Approvals		Summarize Hours Worked
FTE = 0.5		FTE = 3.0		FTE = 0.5		FTE = 3.0
OT = 0%		OT = 20%		OT = 5%		OT = 10%
Errors = N/A		Errors = 15%		Errors = 10%		Errors = 7%

	8 hours		6 hours		2 hours	
1 hour		4 hours		0.5 hours		4 hours

TT = 8 hrs	TT = 5.5 hrs	TT = 1.5 hrs
IQT = 0 hrs	IQT = 0.5 hrs	IQT = 0.5 hrs

Terms:	
FTE = Full time equivalent	TT = Transit time
OT = overtime	IQT = inbound queue time

Given the issues shown in the map, it would be reasonable to implement a more auto-mated method of time tracking, such as a computerized time clock. By doing so, the two bottlenecks in the process can be eliminated, along with overtime and the high error rate. Automation will also likely reduce the total processing time by a substantial amount. The controller might not have realized the severity of the problems with time-keeping without a VSM to clarify the issues.

Consider focusing particular attention on the time periods in a VSM that are be-tween processing steps. The amount of transit and inbound queue time listed in these areas likely exceeds the processing time by an enormous amount, and represents an excellent opportunity for time reduction. In the preceding example, the transit and inbound queue times represent 63% of the total process time. If this slack time can be reduced, the overall capacity of a process increases, which means that fewer resources can be allocated to a process.

Tip: The information in a value stream map is an aggregation of many transactions. If you drill down to individual transactions in a process, you will likely find that about 20% of the transactions cause 80% of the problems, usually because they represent unexpected or unusually complex transactions.

Value stream mapping is an especially effective tool when used to break down the elements of high-volume processes; these processes are completed many times in a typical year, so even small changes can yield large cumulative benefits. Conversely, there is little point in using VSM to analyze tasks that require little time and are only rarely completed, since there is only a modest opportunity for improvement.

Tip: Errors are more likely when there are long inbound queue times, because the size of the work backlog forces employees to cut corners to complete work in a timely manner.

Summary

Any investigation into quality issues will likely require the use of multiple investiga-tive tools. Pareto analysis should be high on your list of options, since it is useful for identifying those issues that will result in the greatest return on your invested time and funds. Another personal favorite is root cause analysis, since it is useful for drilling down to underlying problems and developing action items in short order.

Chapter 4
Supplier Quality Management

Introduction

A large part of the cost of a manufactured product usually comes from a firm's supplier base. That being the case, it makes sense to ensure that the quality level of goods coming from suppliers is a high as possible. In this chapter, we cover several approaches for ensuring that supplier quality levels are maintained at the highest possible levels.

> **Note:** The following discussion refers to the goods and services that go into a buyer's products, not the general supplies (such as cleaning products) that are used in general operations. It is rarely cost-effective to apply supplier quality management techniques to the latter items.

Information Requirements

For a supplier to provide a buyer with quality goods, it first needs to understand the buyer's requirements. This means that the buyer must provide the supplier with a comprehensive set of requirements, including special processing instructions, production specifications, and drawings. Furthermore, the buyer should communicate these requirements in sufficient detail that the supplier has a complete understanding of them.

> **Tip:** It can be useful to discuss with a supplier whether a change to the purchase requirements will result in better-quality parts being delivered. This can work well when tight specifications are not really necessary.

If the buyer's products are subject to government regulation or need to be traced for possible future recalls, the supplier needs to know about any associated record keeping requirements. These requirements can be burdensome, so the supplier needs to know before it can formulate a bid. In some cases, the requirements may be so burdensome that the supplier elects not to bid at all.

The buyer may also want to have its own corrective action system installed at the supplier, at least for those processes that manufacture the goods sold to it. This approach is generally not recommended, since it may result in two systems running side-by-side at the supplier location.

In addition, the buyer should enter into an information sharing agreement with the supplier, where the buyer conducts an ongoing evaluation of the supplier's products and performance, and shares this information with the supplier. In addition, the buyer should report to the supplier how its quality level compares to that of other suppliers that provide similar goods and services to the buyer. This information is needed by the supplier to determine whether it needs to take steps to enhance its quality performance. Ideally, a supplier should not be surprised when it is dropped by the buyer, since the reporting system would have made the reasons for doing so quite clear in advance of the decision.

A key element of an information sharing agreement is to communicate back to the supplier the results of an initial inspection of the supplier's delivered goods. This is done so that the supplier has a better knowledge of which product characteristics must be checked. The buyer may want to have staff on-site during these checks, to ensure that they are conducted correctly.

To enhance the information sharing just noted, the buyer should also offer to provide technical advice to the supplier. This is done when suppliers would profit from quality best practices that are being used elsewhere in the buyer's supplier base. The form of assistance may range from a few conference calls to a much more in-depth on-site visit. These assistance offers represent a commitment by the buyer to the supplier, to improve its odds of success in continuing to do business with the buyer.

Supplier Evaluations

When the goods to be acquired from a supplier are of the non-standard variety, it is especially important that the supplier be able to match the buyer's quality standards. This calls for some on-site investigation to answer the following questions:

- What quality-specific processes, review steps, and measurements does the supplier use?
- What inspecting and testing procedures does the supplier use?
- How does the management team respond to identified instances of low quality?
- How does the supplier monitor its level of quality? At what points in the production process are quality reviews completed?
- What is the nature of the supplier's quality information systems?
- Does the organization follow the quality guidelines established for the ISO 9000 certification or the Malcolm Baldrige National Quality Award?

The buyer should then develop a scoring system for judging supplier performance. One option is to use the 0-to-5 point system that appears in the following exhibit, which is then applied to a variety of quality-related investigations.

Point Scoring Logic

Points	Scoring Logic
0	Does not meet any aspect of the requirement
1	Significant issues with meeting the requirement
2	Minor nonconformities in meeting the requirement
3	Adequate ability to meet the requirement
4	Exceeds expectations set by the requirement
5	Best-in-class ability to meet the requirement

In the following exhibit, we show how the 0-to-5 point system can be applied to a supplier evaluation. An actual supplier evaluation would be much longer – we merely show how such an evaluation would be constructed.

Sample Supplier Evaluation

Area of Analysis	Score
A quality system is operational	4
Supplier personnel can identify quality problems	3
Supplier personnel commonly correct identified quality problems	2
There are inspection stations operating within the supplier facility	4
Supplier managers regularly review the status of the quality program	2
Quality records exist and are regularly updated	3
Quality costs are reported to management	3
Changes to process requirements are tightly controlled	0

It is generally better to develop supplier ratings that are broken down into a number of sub-categories, rather than attempting to create a single numerical score. This is because some of the line items in the ranking system are more important than others, and can be lost within a more general ranking score.

The person creating a supplier evaluation should also provide extensive notes about the conditions found, in order to give a more comprehensive view of the quality status of a supplier. If the supplier disagrees with a score, the supplier's position should also be noted within the evaluation.

Another way to evaluate a supplier is to have it submit a few items that have passed its internal quality reviews. If these items also pass the buyer's quality reviews, then it is likely that the outcomes of the two quality systems roughly correlate. If not, then the supplier's quality systems are likely to be sub-standard.

Yet another way to evaluate suppliers is to monitor their performance over time. Usually, a trend of non-conformance will gradually build over time, which can be spotted and communicated back to the supplier for remediation.

Supplier evaluations will continue after a contract has been awarded. The basic assumption is that the processes originally evaluated by the buyer will remain stable, but this is not really the case. The buyer will want to be notified whenever the supplier makes a change to a process, or to its quality program. Or, if there is a subsequent slippage in the quality of delivered goods, then the buyer will likely want to conduct an inspection of these systems.

The Supplier Scorecard

When a buyer enters into a formal relationship with a supplier, it may demand that the supplier agree to a service-level agreement (SLA). An SLA usually states the performance criteria that the buyer expects of the supplier, such as timely deliveries and specific quality levels. These performance criteria are stated as measurements, which are included in a supplier scorecard.

This scorecard is continually compiled by the buyer's internal systems, tracking such measurements as a supplier's fulfillment rate, defect rate, billed price variance, and perfect order percentage. Other quantitative measurements may also apply, or replace the ones noted here – it all depends on the priorities of the company.

It is also possible that qualitative scores may be applied to suppliers, though these measurements are inherently more difficult to compile and are subject to widely-ranging outcomes, depending on who is conducting the scoring. Possible qualitative measures are:

- *Cost management support.* Does a supplier proactively point out ways in which the buyer can reduce its costs? For example, it might point out that less-expensive raw materials could replace the ones being used.
- *General compatibility.* How well do the supplier and the buyer work together? Is this a generally collegial relationship, or is it more adversarial?
- *Problem resolution support.* How quickly does the supplier act to resolve problems as they arise? Is there finger pointing, or does the supplier simply fix whatever issue is brought up?
- *Product development support.* How well does a supplier assist the buyer in its efforts to create new products? Do their engineers attend review sessions? Do they offer the use of their latest intellectual property?

The final scorecard version might present a lengthy list of items on which suppliers are being reviewed. A key issue from the supplier's perspective is figuring out which of these ratings are the most important from the perspective of the buyer. The issue can be resolved by including a weighting for each line item. Those line items assigned a large weighting are more important to the buyer. In the following sample scorecard, the issuing company has decided that on-time delivery is the most important line item to bring to the attention of suppliers, so that criterion has been assigned the largest weighting. The sample scorecard employs a five-point scoring system.

Sample Weighted Scorecard

Performance	Weighting	Score	Weighted Score
Billed price variance	0.5	3	1.5
Cost management support	1.0	1	1.0
Fulfillment rate	1.2	2	2.4
On-time delivery	2.0	4	8.0
Problem resolution support	1.5	5	7.5
Product development support	0.5	1	0.5
Total			20.9

Supplier scorecards may be posted on a secure company website for suppliers to peruse, or they could be transmitted to supplier representatives at regular intervals by email. In cases where the scorecard results are in serious need of improvement, it may be necessary to have a formal meeting to discuss the findings, and how to improve them. From an internal perspective, unusual scorecard results should be sent to purchasing and quality personnel at once, so that indicated issues can be acted upon immediately.

The scorecard should be considered a two-way street – that is, suppliers also need to be able to comment on the buyer's treatment of them. In particular, they may have a valid point that the buyer's actions are causing their performance measurements to look sub-standard. For example, if the buyer is constantly altering its short-term production schedule, this makes it much more difficult for suppliers to meet their on-time performance targets. In order to hear these comments, it is useful to have in-person meetings, to dig into the underlying reasons for problems.

Dealing with Special Processes

A buyer may have to purchase from a supplier that uses a special process for the production of goods. A special process is one for which testing subsequent to processing is not possible. For example, it may not be cost-effective to examine every weld used in the frame of an apartment building. In these cases, the buyer will need to take extra steps to ensure that the supplier carries out all processes correctly. One way to do so is through certification, such as when a welder must hold a current Certified Welder license before being allowed to work on the apartment building in the preceding example. Alternatively, the buyer can certify the process itself. A process certification involves the creation of a procedure that the process must follow, and then inspecting the process to see if it adheres to the procedure.

Tip: It can make sense to hire a consultant with the necessary skills to provide a certification for a special process, since it is likely that the buying organization does not have this expertise in-house.

Supplier Partnerships

The increased emphasis on quality within supplier organizations means that a buying organization needs to invest substantial sums to ensure that upstream quality levels are properly maintained. An obvious outcome of this situation is the need to shrink the supplier base, so that the buyer can reduce its investment in this area. A typical approach is to develop a supplier ranking system, and use the resulting scores to eliminate low-performing suppliers. The purchases made from these suppliers are then shifted to higher-performing suppliers, leading to a gradual concentration of purchases among fewer suppliers. As the buyer begins to rely on fewer suppliers for the bulk of its purchases, it needs to start viewing them as strategic partners that are to be maintained over the long term, rather than commoditized entities that can be readily swapped out.

As suppliers are treated more like partners, the buyer needs to include them in more decisions. This includes how products are to be designed, which components to include in its goods, and the specifications of those components. By being more inclusive in decision-making processes, suppliers are more willing to put the interests of the buyer ahead of its other customers. This can have several positive effects, such as setting aside more of their production capacity for the buyer's use, and being more willing to invest in new tooling that is specific to the buyer's requirements.

In a supplier partnership, it is necessary to broaden the links between the two organizations. Traditionally, only the buyer's salesperson would contact the purchasing agent for the supplier, with all communications channeled through these two parties. It is much more effective for the people throughout each organization to directly interact with their counterparts in the other organization. Thus, product designers for each organization would talk to each other, as would the quality personnel at each organization.

Summary

It is essential to confine supplier quality management practices to just those purchases from which the buyer will profit the most. This means that simple purchases with loose tolerances require no expenditure of time, while purchases that are vital to the quality of the buyer's goods should be the center of attention. This differentiation should result in precise targeting of quality management activities where they are most needed.

When quality management systems are developed with key suppliers, the emphasis should be on the development of trust between the organizations. This means that all issues should be cooperatively resolved, where both parties are working toward a solution that benefits the ultimate customer. The development of trust also mandates that penalties only be imposed when absolutely necessary, and where the supplier understands the reasons for their imposition. These situations call for very high levels of communication, so that issues are both spotted and resolved as quickly as possible.

Chapter 5
Quality Metrics

Introduction

Many metrics can be employed to track quality within all aspects of a business. This does not mean that every possible metric *should* be followed, since doing so might bury an organization in the associated data collection and reporting tasks. Instead, you should consider a range of reporting options, and only select the ones that require a minimal amount of data collection and give a true representation of the quality issues that management wants to monitor. In the following sections, we itemize several quality metrics that might be worth using.

Supplier Performance Index

One way to evaluate suppliers is to base the analysis entirely on cost – including the cost of nonconformance. Doing so removes any subjectivity from an evaluation. Under this approach, called the supplier performance index (SPI), the cost of the purchases from a supplier is combined with all costs of supplier nonconformance, and then divided by the cost of the purchases. The formula is:

$$\frac{\text{Total purchases cost} + \text{Cost of nonconformance}}{\text{Total purchases cost}}$$

The ideal score is 1.0, which only occurs when there are zero nonconforming incidents. Clearly, the entire point of this index is to focus on the cost of nonconformance, which can include many items, including the following:

- Customer returns traced back to the supplier
- Deliveries outside the required delivery window
- Nonconforming goods
- Subsequent rework costs
- Subsequently scrapped materials

This index can be difficult to implement, because the accounting system does not track costs in accordance with the nonconformance events just described. Quite a major overhaul of the accounting system would be required to come anywhere near the requirements of a nonconformance cost tracking system. Instead, it is much simpler to conduct a one-time cost accounting project to develop a standard cost for each of these nonconforming events, and then assign this cost to each identified event. By doing so, the SPI database can be kept largely separate from the accounting system.

EXAMPLE

The purchasing department of Luminescence Corporation is developing a system to track the supplier performance index of its suppliers. All exception conditions are noted in a database, which automatically creates a cost of nonconformance based on a standard cost per type of event. The system also pulls in the total purchases cost from the purchase orders file maintained by the department. The nonconformance calculation for one of its suppliers is:

Nonconformance Event	Number of Events	Standard Event Cost	Extended Cost of Nonconformance
Customer returns caused by supplier	4	$3,000	$12,000
Deliveries outside delivery window	12	500	6,000
Nonconforming goods	9	425	3,825
Rework	2	175	350
Scrapped materials	--	--	1,700
Total			$23,875

The scrapped materials line item does not show a standard cost, because Luminescence has a separate cost tracking system for scrap. The system nets the cost of scrapped materials against the revenue gained from selling the items for metal scrap. The scrap figure traced to the supplier is included in the table.

During the measurement period, Luminescence purchased $500,000 of goods from the supplier. The resulting SPI is calculated as follows:

$$\frac{\$500,000 \text{ Total purchases cost} + \$23,875 \text{ Cost of nonconformance}}{\$500,000 \text{ Total purchases cost}}$$

$$= 1.048$$

The amount of the index was strongly influenced by the total purchases cost. If the amount purchased had been twice as large, the index would have declined to 1.024. Conversely, if the amount purchased had been half the amount, the index would have increased to 1.096.

Some of the standard event costs noted in the example might appear to be unusually high. This is not the case, for a nonconformance event can have broad (and expensive) ramifications for a business. For example, a late delivery may trigger a production line stoppage or the use of air freight to bring in alternative goods from a different supplier. Even worse, a customer return can trigger the scrapping of the returned product, as well as a damaged relationship with the customer.

Tip: Share with suppliers the standard cost of nonconformance. This gives them a better idea of the costs incurred by the company, and can drive them to further improve their performance.

The SPI is particularly useful when a company is already doing business with several suppliers, and wants to determine which one actually costs the least. It is entirely possible that a comparison of their SPIs will reveal that the supplier charging the lowest cost per unit is actually more expensive than another supplier, because it has shaved its costs so much that it is unable to meet the company's performance criteria, and so continually experiences nonconforming events.

Supplier Defect Rate

Another element of supplier performance is whether they can deliver goods that are free of defects. The concept of defectiveness means that the delivered goods meet the specifications set by the buyer. Thus, if the buyer sets unusually tight tolerances for a component, and the supplier delivers goods that are considered acceptable for general usage but which do not fit the buyer's tolerance limits, then those goods are considered to be defective. Defective components are an especially pernicious problem in a just-in-time manufacturing environment, for there may be no buffer stock on hand to prevent production from stopping if a part proves to be defective.

To measure the defect rate, divide the total number of rejected components by the total number of components received from a supplier during the measurement period. The formula is:

$$\frac{\text{Total number of rejected units}}{\text{Total number of units received}}$$

Defect rates are one of the more important ways in which to evaluate a supplier, so consider breaking down the measurement in several ways, such as by individual part, by supplier facility, by defect type, and by the trucking firm used to deliver the goods – in short, in any way that can yield insights into the reasons for defects or damage.

One problem with this measurement is that it may not be possible to detect defects in the receiving area; problems may not become apparent until later. In this case, a measurement option is to continue tracing product quality back to suppliers as items move through the production process and on to customers. Ultimately, it may be necessary to tie field failure rates back to suppliers. If the last approach is used as a measurement, a possibility is to create a comparison of field failures to the total installed population of a product. The formula is:

$$\frac{\text{Field failures}}{\text{Total installed population}}$$

Another issue to be aware of is increases or decreases in the defect rate that are caused by changes in the company's threshold tolerance limits. If these limits are relaxed, then the defect rate will improve, and vice versa – and without any change in supplier performance. Thus, it is useful to lock down the tolerance limits over multiple reporting periods, if the supplier defect rate is being measured on a trend line. Otherwise, there will be unusual spikes and declines in the reported defect rate that have nothing to do with the supplier.

EXAMPLE

Billabong Machining Co. manufactures high-tolerance widgets for the military market. These combat-ready widgets must be exactly ¼" thick. In recent months, the receiving department has rejected a substantial number of deliveries from the company's steel plate supplier, because the delivered plates have been as much as 1/8" thinner than specified in the authorizing master purchase order. This has resulted in several late widget deliveries to the military, and a threatened cancellation of the company's sole source contract with the military. Accordingly, Billabong's purchasing manager prepares the following defect rate table, which clearly shows how the problem has increased over the past three months:

	January	February	March
Rejected plate deliveries	5	10	15
Total plate deliveries	55	50	60
Supplier defect rate	9%	20%	25%

The purchasing manager uses this table as the basis for a difficult discussion with the steel plate supplier, to either upgrade its performance or be dropped as a preferred supplier.

Yield Measurements

A key element of the profitability of a manufacturing operation is its ability to produce goods without error. Otherwise, the operation may incur extremely high costs related to wasted raw materials, machine usage, and rework. The following two measurements focus on yield, which is the ability to produce the expected number of units.

First-Pass Yield

A potentially massive amount of additional work is required in the production area when goods cannot be manufactured correctly on the first pass. These costs include the repurchase of raw materials to create replacement goods, as well as rework for those items that can be recovered. Management can focus on the measurement of first-pass yield on the most troublesome work stations on a continuing basis, so that issues are continually highlighted and corrected.

To measure first-pass yield, divide the number of units successfully completed by a manufacturing process by the total number of units initiated. The formula is:

$$\frac{\text{Number of units successfully completed}}{\text{Number of units initiated}}$$

EXAMPLE

The owner of Smithy Ironworks is annoyed that so many of the iron garden curios produced by the company are found to have flaws, and must be melted down for recasting. The owner closely follows the first-pass yield, which highlights the following problems with the company's casting process:

Number of units initiated	10,000
- Mold damage	-237
- Incorrect furnace temperature	-150
- Defective iron ore	-80
- Improper finishing	-270
First-pass yield	9,263

The first-pass yield is 92.6%. Based on the volume of errors, the owner elects to focus on improper finishing issues in more detail.

Material Yield Variance

The material yield variance is the difference between the actual amount of material used and the standard amount expected to be used, multiplied by the standard cost of the materials. The formula is:

(Actual unit usage - Standard unit usage) × Standard cost per unit

An unfavorable variance means that the unit usage was greater than anticipated.

The standard unit usage is developed by the engineering staff, and is based on expected scrap rates in a production process, the quality of raw materials, losses during equipment setup, and related factors.

EXAMPLE

The engineering staff of Hodgson Industrial Design estimates that eight ounces of rubber will be required to produce a green widget. During the most recent month, the production process used 315,000 ounces of rubber to create 35,000 green widgets, which is nine ounces per product. Each ounce of rubber has a standard cost of $0.50. Its material yield variance for the month is:

(315,000 Actual unit usage - 280,000 Standard unit usage) × $0.50 Standard cost/unit

= $17,500 Material yield variance

There are a number of possible causes of a material yield variance. For example:

- *Scrap*. Unusual amounts of scrap may be generated by changes in machine setups, or because changes in acceptable tolerance levels are altering the amount of scrap produced. A change in the pattern of quality inspections can also alter the amount of scrap.
- *Material quality*. If the material quality level changes, this can alter the amount of quality rejections. If an entirely different material is substituted, this can also alter the amount of rejections.
- *Spoilage*. The amount of spoilage may change in concert with alterations in inventory handling and storage.

Orders Damaged in Transit

A company may think that it has done an excellent job of shipping on time and fulfilling every line item in an order. However, these activities mean little if a customer finds that the goods have been damaged in transit. The result is a flurry of activity to issue a credit to the customer or to deliver a replacement (possibly using an overnight delivery service). The end result is more expense incurred by the seller and an unhappy customer.

To calculate the proportion of orders damaged in transit, divide the number of complaints received regarding damaged goods by the total number of orders shipped. The formula is:

$$\frac{\text{Number of customer complaints regarding damaged goods}}{\text{Total number of orders shipped}}$$

There is generally little time delay between when an order is shipped and when a customer complains about damage, since damage is usually observed as soon as a delivery is opened and inspected. Nonetheless, it is possible that an order recorded at the end of one measurement period will not experience a complaint until the beginning of the next period. To mitigate this issue, use a relatively wide measurement period, such as three months, and adopt it on a rolling basis.

This measurement is only the starting point for a deep analysis into the reasons for product damage. Here are several possible areas in which damage can occur:

- *Product design*. A product may not have been designed in a sufficiently robust manner to withstand the rigors of transport.
- *Components*. Parts included in a product may be failing, which may require re-sourcing the part with a different supplier.
- *Packaging*. The packaging in which a product is shipped may not provide a sufficient buffer from transport movement.
- *Transport*. The transport company may be handling goods excessively, stacking them inappropriately, or using the wrong form of transport.
- *Receiving*. The handling by the customer's receiving department may be damaging goods before they are opened.

In short, damage in transit has a multitude of causes, and so it can require a prolonged amount of effort to understand and correct problems.

EXAMPLE

Country Figurines produces ceramic, hand-painted figurines from the 1800s era. These figurines are fragile, and require special handling. The company suffers from an inordinately high damage rate for shipped goods. A special task force has concluded that there is nothing wrong with the company's packaging or third-party shippers, and turns its attention to the sole remaining issue that could impact damage – the quality of the production process. The team finds that the temperature at which the glaze on the figurines is fired is inconsistent. A temperature that is 30 degrees or more too high makes the ceramic brittle, rendering it five times more likely to break in transit. After a new temperature control system is installed in the company's firing ovens, the before-and-after results of the damage in transit measurement are as follows:

	Before Temperature Control Fix	After Temperature Control Fix
Damaged goods complaints	360	32
Total orders shipped	4,200	4,450
Proportion of orders damaged in transit	8.6%	0.7%

The temperature control issue has eliminated the bulk of the problem, though there appear to still be some residual issues causing a small number of breakage problems.

Warranty Claims Percentage

A customer may choose to return a product for a variety of reasons, many of which can be traced to other parts of a business than the design of a product. Nonetheless, product design is the core reason for a product return, for the design stage impacts the following:

- The robustness of the product, which impacts its ability to survive transport to the customer location, as well as its subsequent usage.
- The look and feel of the product, which impacts the perceptions of customers regarding the perceived value of goods received.
- The safety of the product, which could fail at an inopportune moment and cause much greater losses for a company than a simple warranty claim.

To calculate the percentage, divide the total number of product claims received by the total number of units sold. An alternative measurement is to divide the replacement cost of warranty claims by the aggregate price of the units sold. The latter approach does a better job of quantifying the cost of warranty claims for the seller.

The two formulas are:

Option One: Option Two:

Number of warranty claims received   Replacement cost of warranty claims
            Number of units sold   Aggregate sales of units sold

Depending on the length of a product's warranty period, there may be a significant time lag between the incurrence of a warranty claim and the original product sale. If so, consider using as the measurement period the length of the standard company warranty. Thus, if the warranty period is six months, the measurement period should be six months on a rolling basis.

EXAMPLE

Green Lawn Care produces electric lawn mowers. The company has been plagued by failed batteries on several of its lawn mower products. In the most recent quarter, the company paid $120,000 for replacement batteries on sales of $2,000,000. The related warranty claims percentage is:

$$\frac{\$120,000 \text{ Replacement cost}}{\$2,000,000 \text{ Sales of units}} = 6\%$$

Transaction Error Rate

It is critical to avoid transaction errors, since the cost of correcting them is several multiples of the cost of initially completing them correctly. Consequently, one of the better measurements is to monitor the transaction error rate. The error rate should be monitored in conjunction with the total number of transactions processed by each person, to see if error rates are higher for newer or less-trained employees. The measurement can be further refined by focusing on those transaction errors that require the most time to repair.

To formulate the transaction error rate, add up all transaction-related errors in a reporting period and divide them by the total number of transactions completed within the same reporting period. This calculation should match transactional errors to the pool of the same types of transactions completed, which will result in a separate error rate for each general type of transaction.

EXAMPLE

The senior payables clerk of the Divine Gelato Company wants to reduce the amount of staff time spent correcting transactional errors. She has derived the following information for the last reporting period:

Processes	Number of Errors	Total Number of Transactions	Transaction Error Rate
Supplier ACH payments	28	3,010	0.9%
Supplier address changes	175	1,390	12.6%
Supplier invoice data entry	200	1,720	11.6%

Based on the error rates of the types of transactions measured, it is evident that the clerk should concentrate her attention on the address changes and invoice data entry. Of these two processes, the one requiring the most effort to repair is invoice data entry, so she elects to begin work in this area.

Additional Quality Metrics

The preceding metrics can form the foundation for a solid quality measurement platform. However, there may be cases in which management wants to conduct more detailed investigations into certain functional areas of a business. If so, we provide the following additional measurement options:

Accounting and Finance Metrics

Billings issued without errors
Payments issued without errors
Percentage of payroll errors
Number of errors in financial statements
Percentage of errors in travel advances issued
Percentage of errors in garnishments
Speed to process expense reimbursements
Time to process credit requests
Time to issue billings
Number of double payments issued to suppliers

Customer Satisfaction Metrics

Customer satisfaction index, covering such matters as service, delivery, and responsiveness
Customer complaints received
Customer quote efficiency, covering the days to process
Customer order entry efficiency, covering the days to process

Customer delivery efficiency, covering delivery timeliness, early deliveries, and late deliveries
Customer order cycle time
Customer reject rates
Customer invoicing errors

Engineering Metrics

Percent of errors found during design review
Time required to make an engineering change
Cost of engineering changes per month
Cycle time to correct customer problems
Percentage of bills of material released in error

Production Control Metrics

Percent of jobs completed on schedule
Percent of errors in purchase requisitions
Percent of time production is down due to stockouts
Cost of rush shipments
Percent of stock errors
Cost of inventory spoilage
Number of bill of lading errors

Purchasing Metrics

Errors per purchase order
Number of unauthorized deliveries received
Percent of incoming deliveries received on time
Expeditors per direct employees
Percent of suppliers with 100% lot acceptance
Purchase order cycle time
Average time to fill emergency orders
Average time to replace rejected lots with good parts
Percent of lots received late
Percent of defect-free supplier parts
Cost of rush shipments

Quality Assurance Metrics

Number of errors detected during design and review analyses
Number of quality assurance audits performed on schedule
Percent of quality inspectors to manufacturing direct labor
Number of engineering changes after design review
Number of process changes after process qualification
Percent of lots going directly to stock
Number of production interruptions caused by supplier parts
Percent of product cost related to appraisal, scrap, and rework
Percent of qualified suppliers

Summary

A well-run system of quality metrics is important, so that management has a feedback loop that shows the outcome of its quality management system. A good starting point for this system is the measurement of suppliers, since they provide such a high percentage of the materials used by most organizations. Some type of yield analysis will also be needed by manufacturing entities, while all organizations should have metrics for warranty claims and transaction error rates.

Quality metrics will only be used if they are reliable. This means that the same calculation must be used for them in every reporting period without exception, so that measured outcomes can be compared across periods. In addition, the method used to collect quality-related data must be consistently applied and stored, in order to obtain consistent results across periods. If a measurement or data collection method is changed, then the change should be rolled back to all reporting periods still being reported to management for comparison purposes.

Glossary

A

Acceptance sampling. A quality control measure that allows you to determine the quality of an entire batch by testing randomly-selected samples and using statistical analysis.

Appraisal costs. The costs of inspection needed to reduce the risk of sending defective products to customers.

B

Business process diagram. A chart that graphically depicts the flow of a business process.

C

Cause-and-effect diagram. A visual layout of the possible causes of a problem.

Control chart. A statistical control used to analyze process variables and monitor their effects on performance.

E

External failure costs. The costs associated with defective products that are uncovered subsequent to delivery to customers.

F

Frequency distribution. A data set that is organized to show the frequency of occurrence of each possible outcome of a repeatable event.

I

Inadvertent error. An error due to a lack of attention.

Internal failure costs. The costs associated with defective products that are uncovered prior to delivery to customers.

K

Kaizen. A continuous improvement process that targets small, incremental enhancements to existing processes.

M

Mean. The average of a group of numbers.

Median. The amount of the middle number in a sorted list of numbers, so that half the data in the sample are above the median and half are below it.

Mode. The cluster of numbers in a group of numbers that occurs most frequently.

P

P-chart. An attributes control chart used with data collected from batches of varying sizes.

Pareto analysis. A method of analysis based on the concept that 20% of the variables included in an analysis are responsible for 80% of the results.

Preventive costs. Costs incurred to avoid product failures.

Process control. The collection of data about a process, from which out-of-control situations can be detected.

Q

Quality. The deficiency-free conformance of a product to the requirements for it.

Quality of conformance. The ability of a company to produce a product that conforms to the original product design.

Quality of design. The ability of a company to design a product that conforms to the quality expectations of a customer.

R

Root cause analysis. A process used to identify the root cause of a problem by asking the question "why" multiple times.

S

Standard deviation. A measure of the amount of variation or dispersion of a set of values.

T

Technique error. When an employee uses an improper technique as part of a process.

Throughput. The number of units that pass through a process over a period of time.

Total quality control. A broad-ranging set of techniques that are employed to minimize errors throughout an organization.

V

Variance. The difference between an expected value and an actual value.

W

Willful error. When someone intentionally causes an error.

Index

www.ingramcontent.com/pod-product-compliance
Lightning Source LLC
Chambersburg PA
CBHW051423200326
41520CB00023B/7339